Experiments for Future STEM Professionals

EXPERIMENTS FOR FUTURE ENGINEERS

ROBERT GARDNER
AND JOSHUA CONKLIN

Enslow Publishing
101 W. 23rd Street
Suite 240
New York, NY 10011
USA
enslow.com

Published in 2017 by Enslow Publishing, LLC.
101 W. 23rd Street, Suite 240, New York, NY 10011

Library of Congress Cataloging-in-Publication Data

Names: Gardner, Robert, 1929- author. | Conklin, Joshua, author.
Title: Experiments for future engineers / Robert Gardner and Joshua Conklin.
Description: New York, NY : Enslow Publishing, 2017. | "2017 | Series: Experiments for future STEM professionals | Includes bibliographical references and index.
Identifiers: LCCN 2015046102 | ISBN 9780766078536 (library bound)
Subjects: LCSH: Engineering—Experiments—Juvenile literature. | Physics—Experiments—Juvenile literature. | Simple machines—Experiments—Juvenile literature. | Science projects—Juvenile literature.
Classification: LCC Q182.3 .G354 2017 | DDC 620.0078—dc23
LC record available at http://lccn.loc.gov/2015046102

Printed in the United States of America

To Our Readers: We have done our best to make sure all website addresses in this book were active and appropriate when we went to press. However, the author and the publisher have no control over and assume no liability for the material available on those websites or on any websites they may link to. Any comments or suggestions can be sent by e-mail to customerservice@enslow.com.

Photo Credits: Cover, Lane Oatey/Blue Jean Images/Getty Images (engineer), Monty Rakusen/Cultura/Getty Images (pipe background throughout book), Alexandr III/ Shutterstock.com (gears symbol), elic/Shutterstock.com (orange geometric background throughout book), Zffoto/Shutterstock.com (white textured background throughout book).

Illustrations by Joseph Hill.

CONTENTS

INTRODUCTION

WHAT DO ENGINEERS DO?

Engineers solve problems. From making a rocket more aerodynamic to refining the design and function of computer screens; engineers use science, mathematics, economics, and countless other tools to meet the needs of the public and private sectors. Engineers work within a variety of frameworks, including budget and scope, to create the products we use every day.

If you think you may have an interest in studying engineering in college, it is important to get started in high school. Your courses should include four years of mathematics and science as well as English and social studies. Looking for opportunities to learn more about engineering outside the classroom (by reading books like this, visiting engineering museums, or mentoring with a current engineer) will also be helpful.

Most successful engineers are creative, analytical, inquisitive, and detail oriented. The best engineers also communicate their thoughts and ideas clearly, both orally and in writing. If you have these abilities and like to solve problems, then a career in engineering might be for you!

TYPES OF ENGINEERING

Engineers work in a variety of fields, helping to build computers, cars, and even cities. They also make systems run more efficiently and products easier to use. You don't have to decide exactly what kind of engineering you'd prefer right now, as many of the necessary skills overlap. However, it is helpful to think about the fields in which you are most interested. The following are brief descriptions of different types of engineering. You can also find more information about engineering careers in the "Career Information" section at the end of this book.

- **Aerospace engineers** are truly rocket scientists. They design, test, and oversee the manufacture and development of airplanes, satellites, rockets, and spacecraft. Their creations may travel to the moon, asteroids, Mars, and beyond.
- **Agricultural engineers** design and develop better machines and procedures for farming and aquaculture. They find more efficient ways to grow and process food, while reducing pollution and conserving vital resources such as water and soil.

- **Biomedical engineers** are involved in designing and making artificial limbs, as well as machines and software used to analyze and diagnose medical issues. Their work helps doctors and medical professionals most effectively diagnose and treat a variety of diseases and conditions.
- **Chemical engineers** use their knowledge of science and mathematics to solve problems related to the production and testing of chemicals, fuels, foods, medicines, and a variety of other products.
- **Civil engineers** research, design, and oversee the construction of projects involving bridges, roads, and tunnels, as well as water and sewage treatment plants. They work to make cities more comfortable to live in, and research designs that make day-to-day life easier.
- **Computer hardware engineers** design, develop, and oversee the manufacture of data networks and electronic devices. They integrate the electronic hardware with developments in computer software and may also be involved with computer programming and the testing of programming code.
- **Computer software engineers** develop the programs that control the operation of your computer software, including word processors and games. They also find and remove computer problems, such as 'bugs,' design and build websites, create computer games, and design and develop apps.
- **Environmental engineers** design and implement ways to solve environmental problems. They improve

recycling practices and find ways to reduce air and water pollution. They also help research and combat major environmental issues such as global warming, water safety and shortages, and waste management.

- **Geological engineers** use their knowledge of geology to search for and evaluate sites where minerals such as copper, coal, and gold might be mined. They also design plans to extract the minerals safely and efficiently.
- **Industrial engineers** design methods to produce a product or a service efficiently and safely, transfer materials to customers profitably, and evaluate ways to improve work efficiency and production.
- **Materials engineers** deal with substances at the atomic level to help solve problems in the manufacturing, testing, and processing of such materials as ceramics, metals, plastics, and electronics.
- **Mechanical engineers** design, build, and test mechanical items such as tools, engines, and all kinds of machines including automobiles, turbines, and robots.
- **Nuclear engineers** research and develop ways to use the vast energy in the nuclei of radioactive atoms. This research can do things as diverse as improving medicine, powering submarines, or making nuclear fusion more efficient.
- **Petroleum engineers** figure out how to best extract oil and gas from deposits below Earth's surface. They also develop new methods to remove more of the oil or gas found in these deposits.

BEFORE YOU BEGIN: SOME SUGGESTIONS

As you do the experiments, demonstrations, and other activities in this book, you may need the help of a partner. It would be best to partner with someone who also enjoys experiments and discoveries in order to get the most enjoyment from your work. **If there are any safety issues involved in doing an experiment, you will be warned. In some cases, to avoid danger, you will be asked to work with an adult. It is imperative that you heed any noted cautions and know that a safe workplace is an essential part of any engineering career**. Don't take any chances that could lead to an injury and if you are unsure, ask an adult.

Like any good engineer, you will find it useful to record your ideas, notes, data, and conclusions in a notebook. By doing so, you keep track of the information you gather and the conclusions you reach. It will allow you to refer to experiments you have completed and help you during future projects. It may also come in handy during college or job interviews as a point of reference.

THE SCIENTIFIC METHOD

Scientists and engineers observe their surroundings and seek to understand how things work. They ask questions, make careful observations, and conduct research. Different areas of science and engineering take different approaches to challenges and, depending on the problem, one method is often better than another. Designing a new artificial heart, building a highway, or constructing a computer game require different methods and techniques, but they all require capable engineers.

Despite the differences, all scientists and engineers approach experiments with the same basic set of rules, called the scientific method. In most experiments, some or all of the following steps are used: making an observation, formulating a question, making a hypothesis (one possible answer to the question) and a prediction (an if-then statement), designing and conducting one or more experiments, analyzing the results in order to reach conclusions about your prediction, and the acceptance or rejection the hypothesis. Scientists and engineers also share their findings by writing articles or giving talks about their experiments and results. Their writings are reviewed by other scientists before being published in journals for wider circulation.

You might wonder where and how to begin an experiment. Simply observe the world around you with a scientist's curiosity. Your observations may then result in a question, which could arise from an earlier experiment or from reading, and may then be answered by a well-designed investigation. Once you have a question, your job is to make a hypothesis, which is a possible answer to the question (what you think will happen). Once you have a hypothesis, it is time to design an experiment to test a consequence of your hypothesis.

In most cases, the investigator conducts what is called a controlled experiment. This means having two groups that are treated exactly the same except for the single factor being tested. That factor is called a variable. For example, suppose you have the question: "Is water less dense than cooking oil?" You might use a balance and a graduated cylinder to investigate. You could weigh 100 milliliters of water and then weigh an equal volume of cooking oil at the same temperature as the water.

During the experiment, you would collect data, observing and recording the mass and volume of each liquid. You would then divide the mass of each liquid by its volume. By comparing the quotients, that is, the densities, you would then draw a conclusion.

Two other terms are often used in scientific experiments—dependent and independent variables. The dependent variable ***depends*** on the value of the independent variable. Here, the dependent value is the mass of the liquids. It depends on the volume, which is the independent variable in this experiment. After the data is collected, it is analyzed to see if it supports or rejects the hypothesis. The results of one experiment often lead you to related questions. Whatever the results, something can be learned from every experiment.

SAFETY FIRST

Safety is imperative in science and engineering! Certain rules apply when conducting experiments. Some of the rules below may seem obvious, others may not, but it is important that they are all followed. Any workplace involving science or engineering will have a similar code of conduct. It is best to start learning how to work like an engineer now.

1. Have an adult help you whenever this book, or any other, advises.
2. Wear eye protection and closed-toe shoes (not sandals).
3. Tie back long hair.
4. Do not eat or drink while experimenting. Never taste substances being used (unless instructed to do so).
5. Do not touch chemicals with your bare hands. Use tools, such as spatulas, to transfer chemicals from place to place.
6. The liquid in some thermometers is mercury (a dense liquid metal). It is dangerous to touch mercury or breathe mercury vapor. Mercury thermometers have been banned in many states. When doing experiments that require you to measure temperature, use only electronic or non-mercury thermometers, such as those filled with alcohol. If you have a mercury thermometer in the house, **ask an adult** if it can be taken to a local thermometer exchange location.
7. Do only those experiments that are described in this book or those that have been approved by **an adult**.
8. Maintain a serious attitude while conducting experiments. Never fool around or play practical jokes.

9. Before beginning an experiment, read and understand all the instructions.
10. Remove all items not needed for the experiment from your work space.
11. At the end of every activity, clean all materials used and store them in a safe location. Then wash your hands thoroughly with soap and water.

The chapters that follow contain experiments and information that every young future engineer should know. They will also help you to decide if engineering is a career you would like to pursue. Good luck and get to work!

CHAPTER ONE

A SIMPLE MACHINE: THE LEVER

You might say machines are an engineer's best friend. Engineers build new machines, improve old machines, and use machines in their everyday work. One of the most common machines is the lever, which is a "simple" machine. Simple machines make work easier to perform or change the direction or size of a force (a push or pull).

There are three kinds of levers—first class, second class, and third class. Let's begin by experimenting with a first-class lever.

EXPERIMENT 1

A FIRST-CLASS LEVER

A lever is a bar or rod, such as a crowbar or seesaw, that can be used to lift things. To lift a load, *L* (like a person or object), a force, *F*, is applied to the lever. The lever turns on a fulcrum or pivot, *P*, as the load, *L*, is lifted.

In a first-class lever, the force and load are at opposite ends of the lever. The fulcrum is between them as shown in Figure 1a. Figure 1b shows a second class lever, and Figure 1c is a diagram of a third class lever.

THINGS YOU WILL NEED

- **2-inch x 6-inch board about 5 feet (1.5 meters) long**
- **1-inch x 1-inch x 12-inch board**
- **a partner**
- **bathroom scale (Many experiments call for a bathroom scale. A non-digital bathroom scale will provide the best results.)**

1. Use the 5 foot (1.5 meter) long board as the lever and the smaller board as the fulcrum, as shown in Figure 2.
2. Ask a partner to sit on the short end of the lever.
3. Push down on the other end of the lever at point 1; then at point 2; and then at point 3. At which point is the least force required to lift your partner? At which point is the largest force required? (You should be able to feel the difference.)
4. Are there points on the lever where you can't lift your partner? If so, where are they?
5. The mechanical advantage (MA) of a machine is defined as the output force divided by the input

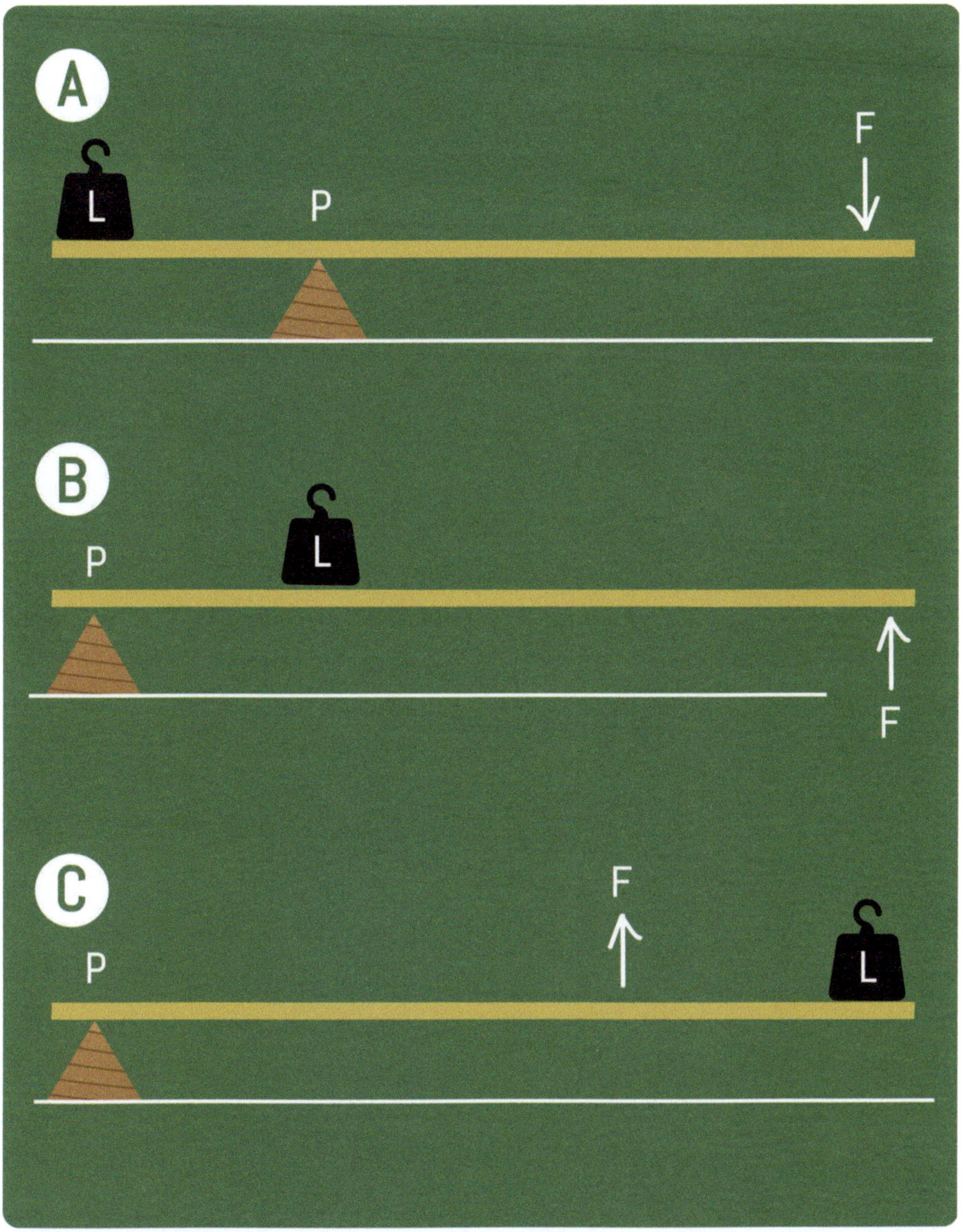

Figure 1. a) A first-class lever. b) A second-class lever. c) A third-class lever.

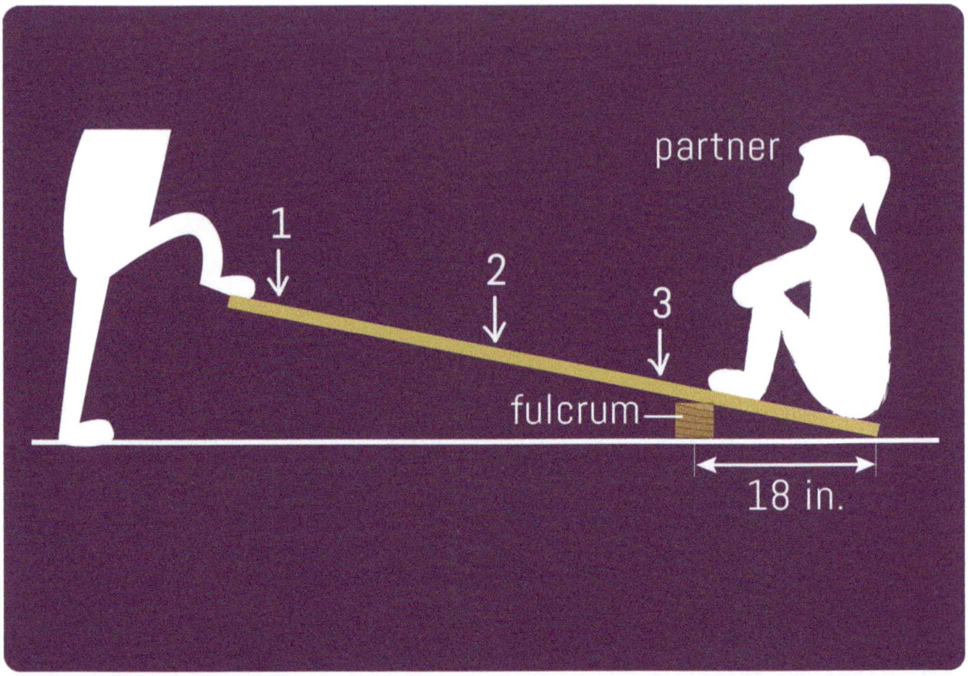

Figure 2. With this lever, the small board is the fulcrum, your partner serves as the load to be lifted, and you provide the force to lift the load.

force, or the load divided by the force used to lift the load.

6. Use a bathroom scale to measure the weight of your partner. Then, placing the scale between your foot and the lever, use the scale to measure the force you used to lift him or her when you pushed at position 1. What was the mechanical advantage?

Will the mechanical advantage be more or less if you push at position 2? Position 3? Make a prediction, then test your prediction by applying the force at position 2 and position 3.

MACHINES AND WORK

As you saw in the previous experiment, machines can be used to make work easier. But what exactly is "work"?

Scientists define work as a force (a push or a pull) times the distance through which the force acts. It can be expressed mathematically as:

Work = force × distance, or simply as,

$$W = f \times d.$$

Suppose you lifted a five-pound bag of flour to a height of three feet. You must lift with a force equal to the weight of the flour (5 pounds). So the work you did was 15 foot-pounds.

W = 5 pounds × 3 feet = 15 foot-pounds or 15 ft-lbs.

In the metric system, which is used by most scientists and some engineers, weight is measured in newtons and distance in meters. Five pounds is approximately 22 newtons and 3 feet is about 0.91 meter. So the work done if measured in the metric system would be:

22 N × 0.91 m = 20 N-m or 20 joules. (A joule of work or energy is equal to one newton-meter)

EXPERIMENT 2

WORK, FORCE, AND FRICTION

If you've ever slid into second base or slid a shaker of salt across a table, you've seen friction in action. Friction is a force that occurs when two surfaces rub against one another. Let's see how it affects machines.

THINGS YOU WILL NEED

- **children's wagon**
- **smooth level surface**
- **rope or clothesline**
- **bathroom scale (non-digital scale will work best)**
- **concrete block or other heavy object**

1. Turn a children's wagon upside-down on a smooth, level surface such as a driveway or sidewalk. Put a concrete block or other heavy object on the wagon (Figure 3).
2. Put a piece of rope or clothesline through the wagon's handle. Tie the ends of the rope together to make a loop.
3. Put the loop around a bathroom scale.
4. Pull the wagon using the scale to measure the force. What force is needed to move the loaded wagon at a slow, steady speed?

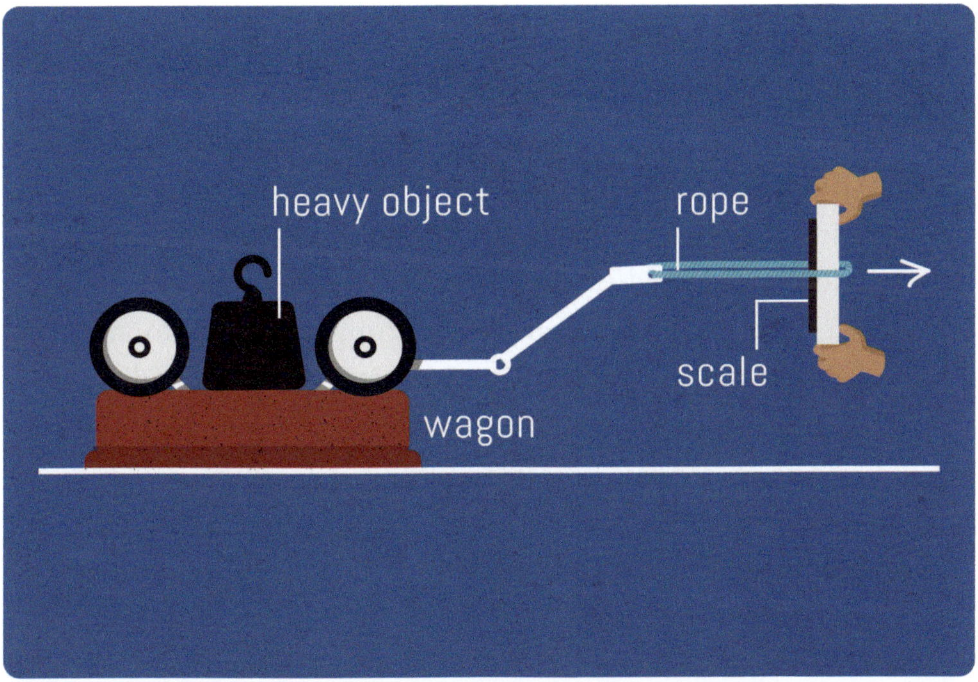

Figure 3. What force is needed to move the wagon at a slow, steady speed?

5. After you pulled the wagon 5 feet, how much work did you do?
6. Now, turn the wagon right-side-up on its wheels. Put the heavy object in the wagon.
7. Pull the wagon using the scale as before to measure the force. How much work did you do this time when you pulled the wagon 5 feet?

Both times you pulled the wagon, you were overcoming friction, which as noted above, occurs when two surfaces rub against one another. It always acts against motion. Friction is present in all machines. Therefore, some work is always needed just to overcome friction.

But as you saw, machines such as wheels can reduce friction. Engineers are always looking for ways to reduce friction and, thereby, work. But frictional forces can never be completely eliminated as long as gravitational forces are present. In satellites orbiting earth, a condition known as weightlessness is present. As you may have seen in television reports on astronauts in spaceships, things can move without friction. However, there will still be friction within the machines functioning in a weightless environment.

SCIENCE, LAWS, AND LEVERS

Scientific laws are based on observations about things and behaviors for which no exceptions have been found. A scientific law is not absolutely certain; in fact scientists are constantly testing laws in an effort to find an exception and disprove the law. In the next experiment you will work with levers to discover a scientific law.

EXPERIMENT 3

LEVERS AND A LAW

Let's see if we can find a rule or law to explain the behavior of levers.

THINGS YOU WILL NEED

- **plastic soda straw**
- **ruler**
- **long pin**
- **2 identical cans or glasses**
- **paperclips**
- **felt-tipped pen**

1. Use a soda straw and a long pin to make an equal-arm lever. The pin will serve as a fulcrum. If the pin (fulcrum) is at the center of the straw, the two equal lengths on either side of the fulcrum make it an equal arm lever.
2. Use a ruler to find the exact middle of the straw. Push the pin through the middle of the straw slightly above its center as shown in Figure 4a.
3. Place the ends of the pin on two identical cans or glasses, also shown in Figure 4a. To see why the pin was inserted above the center, simply turn the straw over. When the pin lies below the straw's center, what happens?

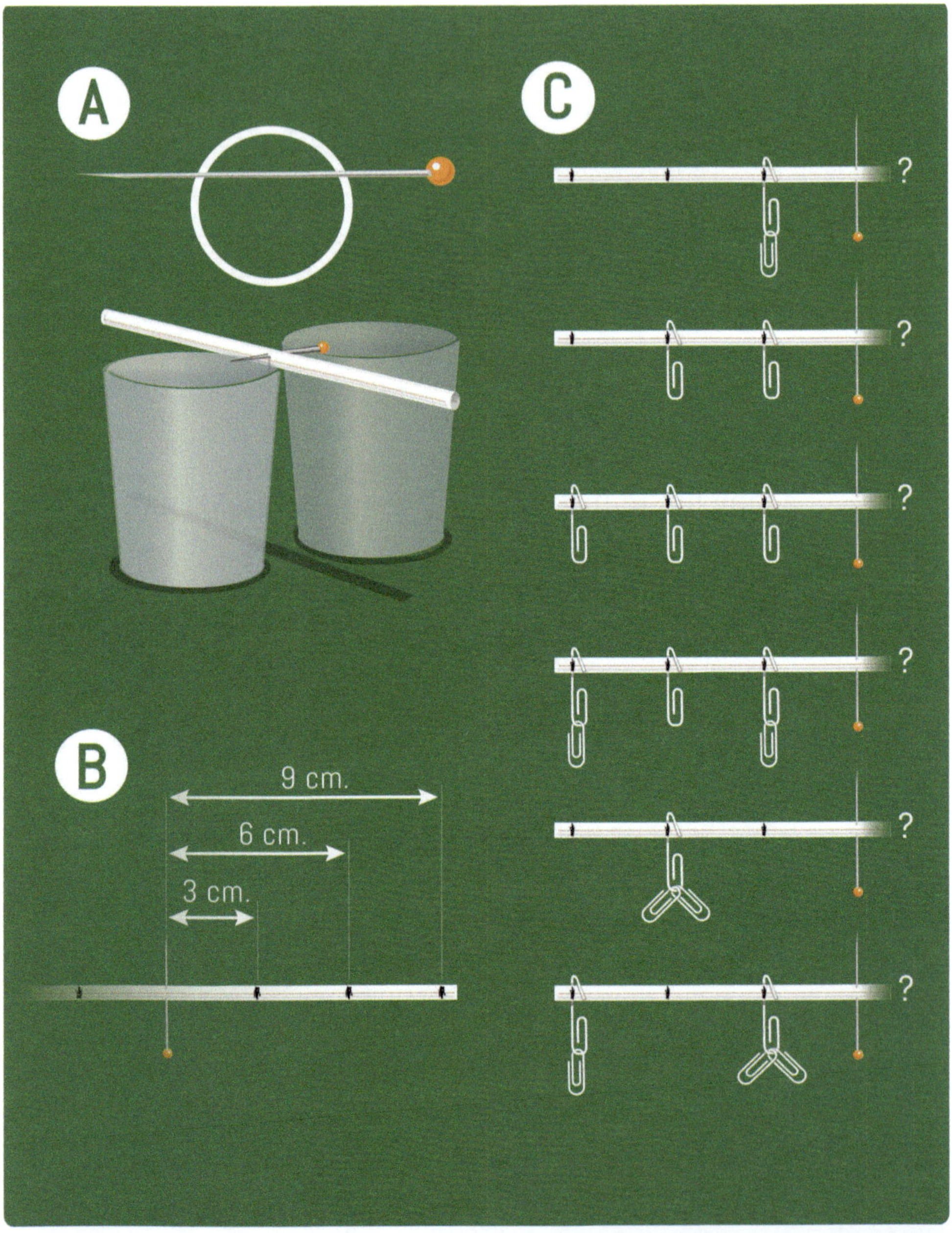

Figure 4. a) The pin should be slightly above the center of the straw.
b) Make marks 3 cm, 6 cm, and 9 cm outward from the midpoint of the straw.
c) Using paper clips on the other side of the lever, how can each of the straws shown here be balanced?

4. Use a felt-tipped pen to make marks at 3 cm, 6 cm, and 9 cm from the pin on both sides of the straw as shown in Figure 4b.
5. Hang a paper clip 9 cm from the pin on one side of the balanced straw. (If the clip slides on the straw, bend it together enough to make it stay in place.) Assuming that all your paper clips have the same weight, where should you place a paperclip on the other side of the straw to make it balance? Where can you place three paper clips on the other side of the lever to make it balance?
6. The drawings in Figure 4c show some arrangements of paper clips on the left side of the straw. For each case shown, how can you balance the straw by adding one or more paper clips to the right side of the straw? In some cases are there more than one way to make it balance? For example, in how many of the cases shown can you balance the straw by using just one paper clip on the right side? Two paper clips on the right side? Three paper clips? Four? More than four?
7. Continue to experiment with your equal-arm soda straw lever using various numbers of paper clips on each side. Can you discover a rule (a law) that enables you to predict a way to always balance the lever?

EXPERIMENT 4

AN UNEQUAL-ARM LEVER

Most levers, like the one you used in Experiment 1, are not equal-arm levers. Let's experiment with a lever that does not have equal arms.

THINGS YOU WILL NEED

- **items from Experiment 3**
- **piece of clay**

1. You can change the equal-arm lever you used in Experiment 3 to an unequal-arm lever. To do this, simply move the support pin (fulcrum) 3 cm to the left of the center position. (See Figure 5a.)
2. The straw will not balance now because more of its weight is to the right of the fulcrum. To make it balance, add a small piece of clay to the left of the fulcrum.

   Which of the arrangements in Figure 5b will balance? Which will not balance?

   Continue to test the unequal-arm lever with different combinations of weights to see if you can discover a law that explains the behavior of levers.

The distance from the fulcrum to the force or weight on the lever is called the *lever arm*. The lever arm times the force is called the *moment of force*. In the experiments you

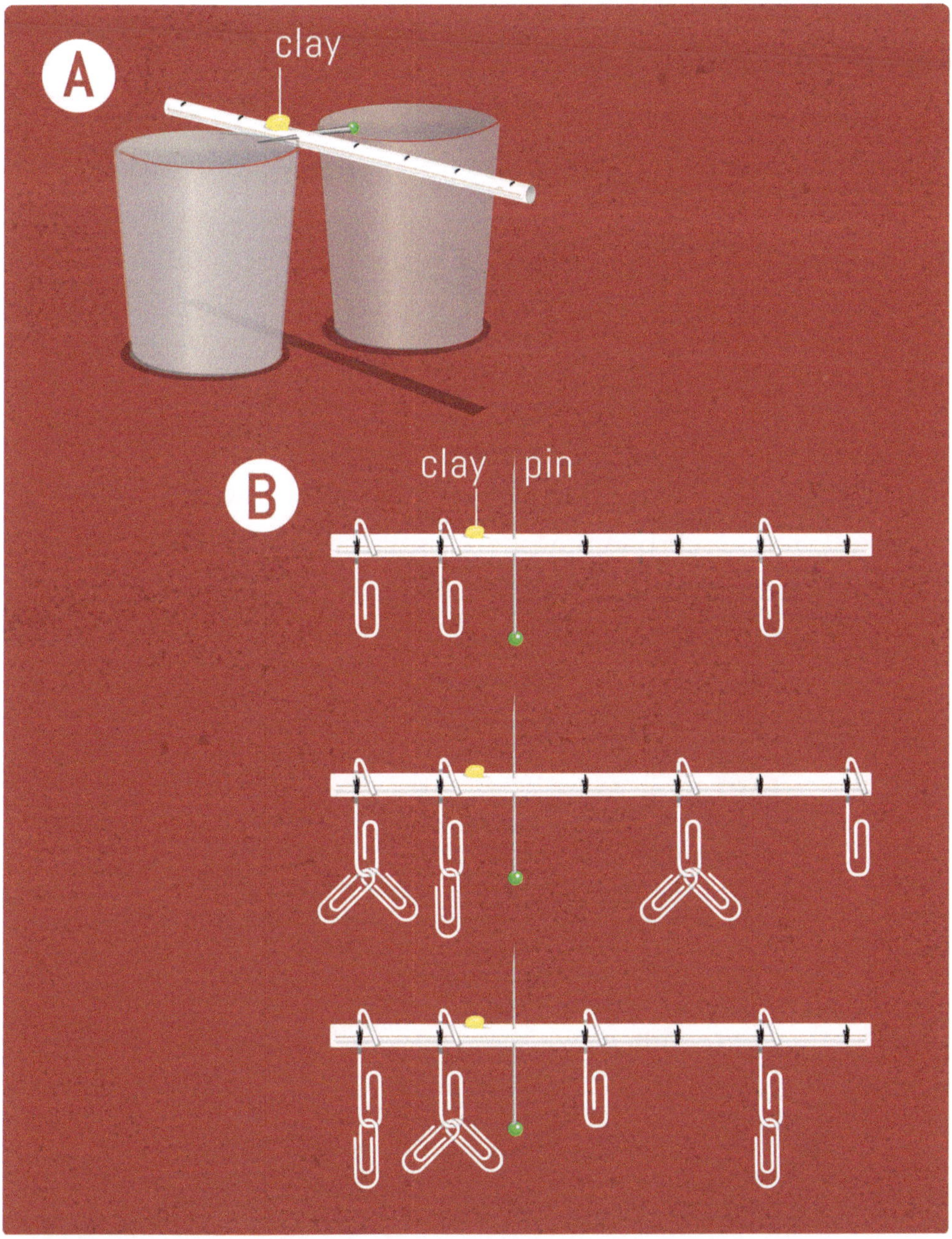

Figure 5. a) Make an unequal-arm lever by moving the pin 3 cm to the left of the straw's midpoint. Does your lever law still hold true? b) Which of the levers shown here will be balanced?

have just done, the moments of force on the right side of the lever tended to turn the lever clockwise. The moments of force on the left side of the lever tended to turn the lever counterclockwise. A paper clip may be considered one unit of weight. For each balanced lever, how did the clockwise moment or moments of force compare with the counter-clockwise moment or moments of force?

EXPLORING ON YOUR OWN

- You use simple levers every time you eat with a knife, fork, and spoon. Make a list of the levers you use every day. Then identify them as first, second, or third class levers.

EXPERIMENT 5

A SECOND-CLASS LEVER

THINGS YOU WILL NEED

- **hammer**
- **small nail**
- **board about 3 feet long and 4 or 5 inches wide**
- **weight, 2–5 pounds (1–2 kilograms)**
- **spring balance**
- **plastic bag**

Let's do an experiment with a second-class lever.

1. Hammer a small nail a short distance into the end of a board about 3 feet long and 4 or 5 inches wide.

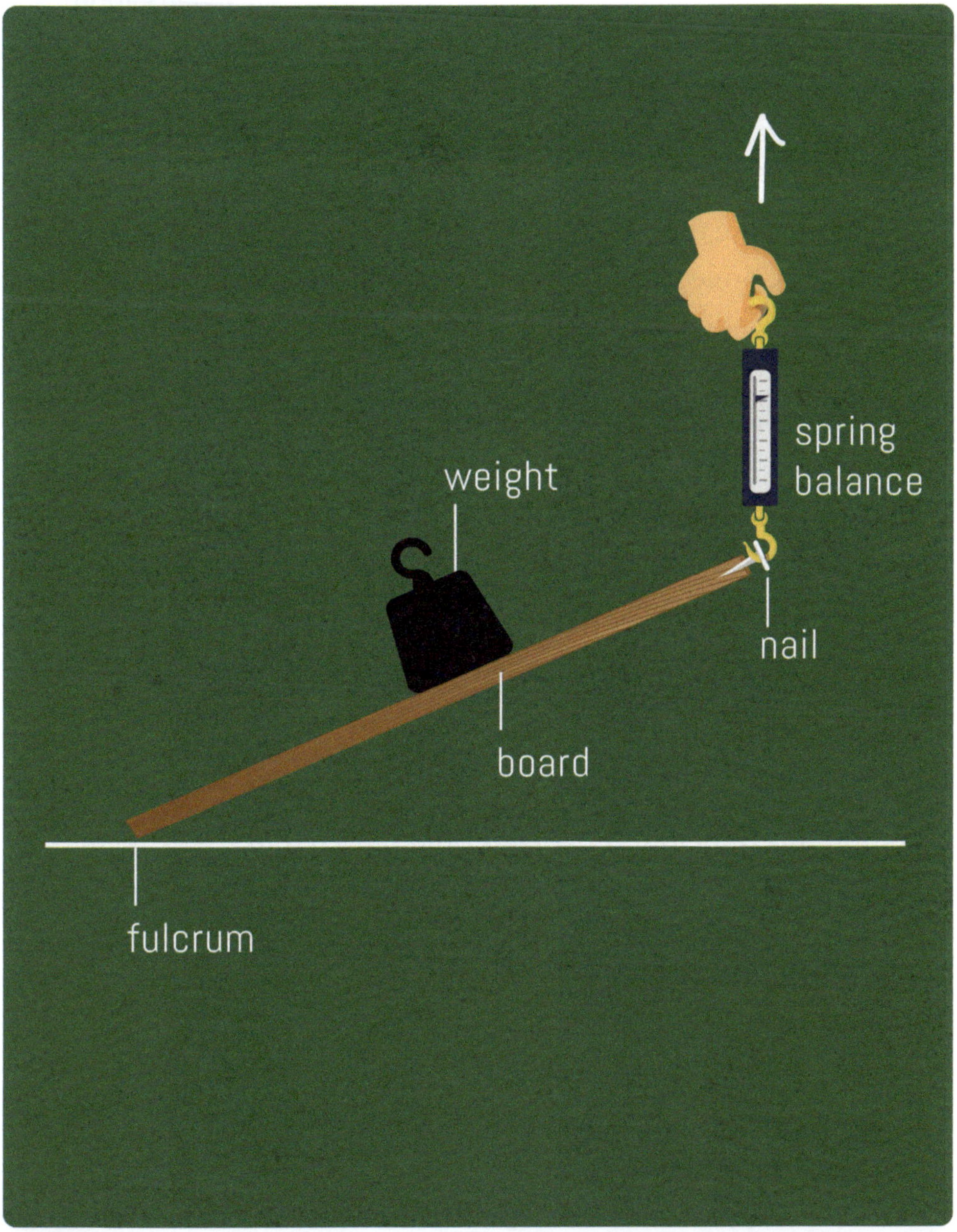

Figure 6. A second-class lever is used to lift a load (weight).

2. Use a can of sand or something else that weighs about 2 to 5 pounds as the load. Weigh the load by placing it in a plastic bag and hanging it from a spring balance. (You can find spring balances online or at many box stores, such as Walmart.) Record its weight. Then place the weight at the center of the board.
3. Connect a spring balance to the nail at the end of the board. Use the other end of the board as the fulcrum. (See Figure 6.) What force is needed to lift the board?

In Experiment 4, you found that the clockwise moments of force were equal to the counterclockwise moments of force when the lever was balanced. Do you find that to be true in this experiment?

WHAT'S WRONG WITH THE LAW?

You probably found the law you discovered in Experiments 3 and 4 did not work in Experiment 5. Is the law wrong, or did you miss something?

When the authors did experiment 5, they weighed the board. And they added the board's weight to the weight placed on the board. When they did this, they found the moments of force (clockwise and counterclockwise) were very nearly the same.

Try this for yourself. Use the sum of the board's weight and the weight you placed on the board when you calculate the moments of force. We think you'll find the clockwise and counterclockwise moments of force are, within experimental error, very nearly the same.

But where did we consider the board's weight to be? Experiment 6 will help answer that question.

EXPERIMENT 6

YOUR CENTER OF MASS

In the previous experiment, we considered the board's weight to be at its middle. We placed the weight to be lifted on the middle as well.

The center of mass of any object is the point where all its mass can be considered to exist. It is also the object's balance point—the point about which the moments of force causing it to rotate in opposite directions are equal. We found the board used in

THINGS YOU WILL NEED

- **padded sawhorse or soft arm of a sofa**
- **meter stick or yardstick**
- **full-length mirror**
- **long, strong, wide board**
- **bathroom scale (A non-digital scale will work best)**
- **a partner**
- **narrow flat stick**
- **short wide board**

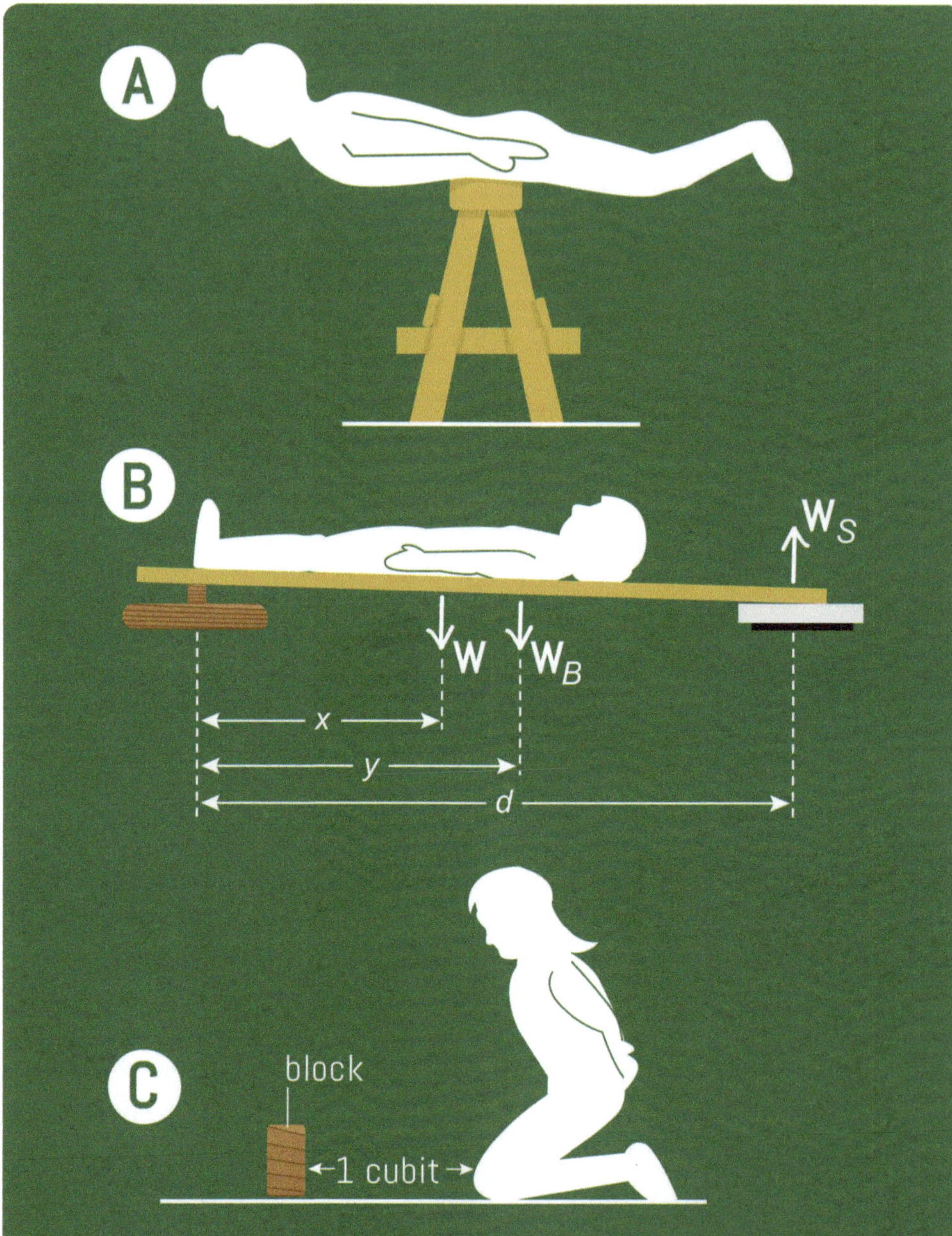

Figure 7. a) You can make a rough approximation of your center of mass by balancing your body on a sawhorse. b) You can more accurately find your center of mass by calculating moments of force. c) Can you knock the block over with your nose?

the previous experiment was balanced when it rested on a fulcrum under its middle.

The center of mass of some objects is easy to find. For example, the center of mass of a sphere, such as a ball, is at its center. The center of mass of a meter stick or a yardstick is at its middle. But what about an object that is less symmetrically built, like a human being? Let's find your center of mass to help us better understand.

You can easily find the approximate location of your center of mass.

1. Lie with your body straight and rigid on a padded sawhorse or the soft arm of a sofa. Either can serve as a fulcrum for your body. Think of your body as an equal-arm balance beam. (See Figure 7a.) When your body is balanced, your center of mass will be directly above the fulcrum.

   What is the approximate location of your center of mass?

   Again, the center of mass of any object is the point where all its mass can be considered to be located. It is also the object's balance point—the point about which the moments of force causing it to rotate in opposite directions are equal.
2. Put your finger under the center of a meter stick or yardstick. Does the stick balance on your finger? What happens if you put your finger under the 40 cm mark? Why do you think this happens?

Like everything else, your body has a center of mass. What will happen if your center of mass is not above your body's points of support (your feet)?

3. To find out, stand with your right leg and shoulder firmly against a wall. What happens when you lift your left foot?
4. Normally, your body automatically adjusts to keep your center of mass above a point of support. To see one way this is done, stand in front of a full-length mirror. Raise your left foot off the floor. How does your body adjust so that your center of mass is above your right foot?

   If you've had some basic algebra, you can find your center of mass quite accurately. To do so you will need a long, strong, uniform board, a fulcrum, and a bathroom scale.
5. Weigh the board by placing it on the bathroom scale. Record its weight.
6. Stand on the scale to find your weight. Record your weight.
7. Place one end of the board on the center of the bathroom scale. Put the other end on a narrow flat stick resting on a wide board. The stick will serve as a fulcrum. The board is the lever.
8. Lie on the board with your feet above the fulcrum as shown in Figure 7b. You now have a second class lever. All your weight, W, can be considered to be

at your center of mass (COM). The board's weight, W_B, and its center of mass can be considered to be at the middle of the board. Your weight and the board's weight create clockwise moments of force about the fulcrum. They are shown as $W \times X$ and $W_B \times Y$ in Figure 7b. The distance from the fulcrum to the board's center of mass is represented by Y. The distance from the fulcrum to your center of mass is represented by X, which is unknown at this point.

9. The counterclockwise moment of force is the force shown on the bathroom scale, W_S, times its distance (d) from the fulcrum, which is $W_S \times d$.
10. Since there is no rotation, the clockwise moments must equal the counterclockwise moments; therefore,

$$(W \times X) + (W_B \times Y) = (W_S \times d).$$

Suppose the board is 7 feet long and weighs 10 pounds, and you weigh 100 pounds. The board's center of mass will be 3.5 feet from the fulcrum. If the scale reads 40 pounds, then:

$$(100 \text{ lb} \times X) + (10 \text{ lb} \times 3.5 \text{ ft}) = 40 \text{ lb} \times 7 \text{ ft}$$

$$100 \text{ lb} \times X + 35 \text{ ft-lb} = 280 \text{ ft-lb}$$

If you subtract 35 lb-ft from both sides of the equation, you have:

$$100 \text{ lb} \times X = 280 \text{ lb-ft} - 35 \text{ lb-ft}$$

$$100 \text{ lb} \times X = 245 \text{ lb-ft}$$

Then, if you divide both sides of the equation by 100 lb, you have:

$$X = 2.45 \text{ ft}.$$

This data would tell you that your center of mass is 2.45 feet (2 ft 13/32 inches) above the bottom your feet, a distance that can be measured.

11. Ask a partner to help you make the actual measurements. Then find your center of mass.
12. Next, lie on the board and raise your arms so that your hands are well above your head. Repeat the experiment in this position. What happens to your center of mass?
13. Find your friend's center of mass using this same experiment. How does your center of mass compare with his or hers?
14. Here's a fun experiment to try. Sit on the floor, resting on your knees. Place a small block upright on its narrow side one cubit in front of your knees. A cubit a distance equal to the length of your forearm (from your elbow to the tip of your longest finger).

    Now put your hands behind your back. Can you, without tipping over, use your nose to tip the block over? (See Figure 7c.)

    Try this with a number of different people. You will probably find that girls and women can do this more easily than men and boys. Can you explain why?

EXPERIMENT 7

A THIRD-CLASS LEVER

THINGS YOU WILL NEED

- **bathroom scale (non-digital scales will work best)**
- **heavy table or counter**
- **pillows, if necessary**
- **small block of wood**
- **cloth**

If you go back and examine Figure 1 you will see a third-class lever does not make work easier. The force, *F*, must be greater than the load being moved because the force is closer to the fulcrum than the load. Nevertheless, a number of simple tools we commonly use are third-class levers. One example of a third-class lever is your forearm. (See Figure 8.)

Based on your knowledge of third-class levers, do you think you could lift more with your fingers, your wrist, or your forearm?

1. To find out, place a bathroom scale against the underside of a heavy table or counter. Let the dial extend out far enough so that you can see it.
2. Sit in front of the scale with your forearm at a right angle and in contact with the scale. (Sit on pillows if necessary.)

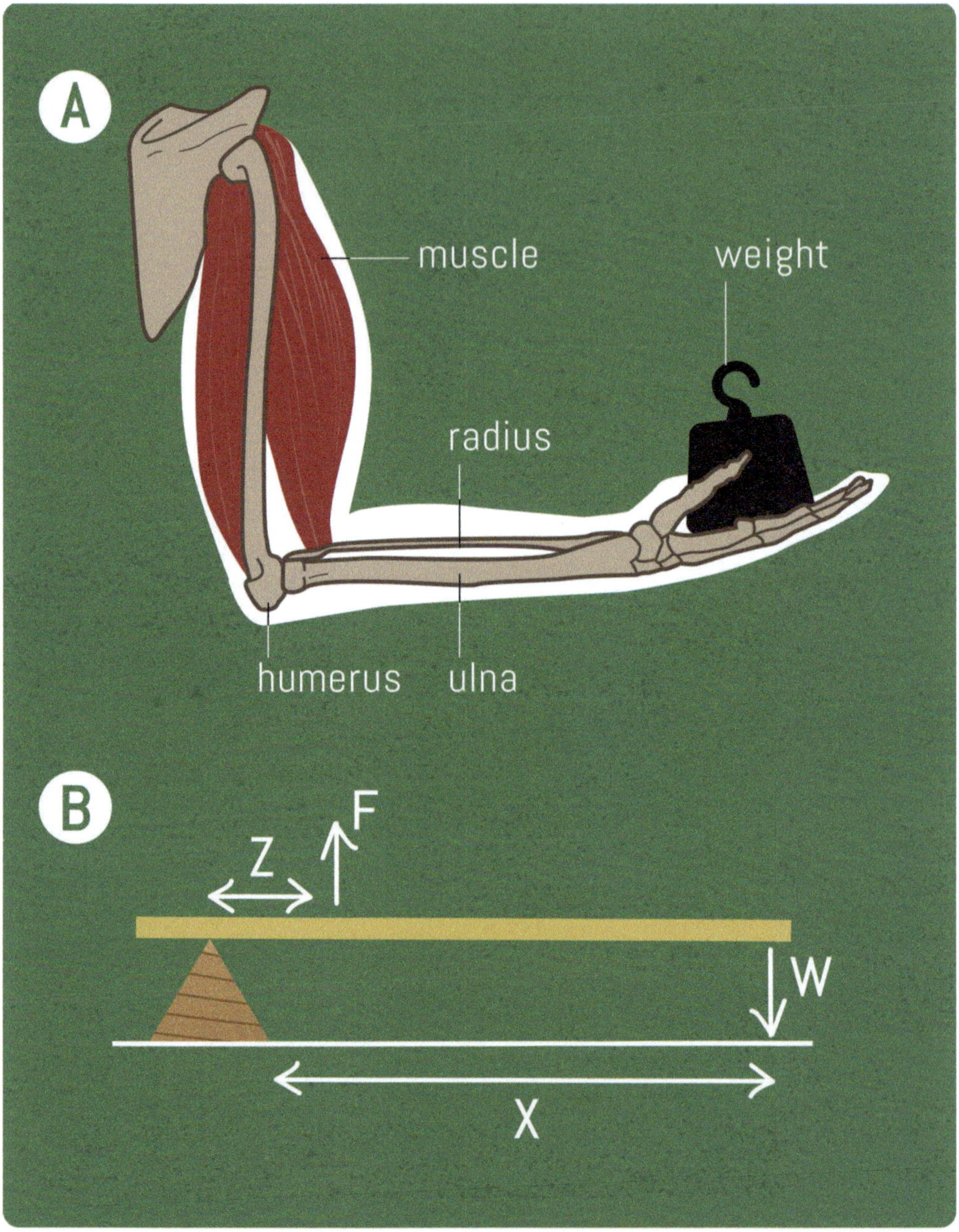

Figure 8. a) The drawing shows how the human forearm acts like a third-class lever when it lifts a weight. b) When the human forearm acts like a third class lever, the biceps muscle pulls upward on the bones of the lower arm (radius and ulna) creating a counterclockwise moment of force, *F* x *Z*. The weight, *W*, times its distance, X, from the elbow or fulcrum, creates a clockwise moment of force, *W* x *X*.

3. Wrap a small block of wood in some cloth. Use the block to push against the scale.
4. Using your fingertips, with how much force can you push upward?
5. Using your wrist, with how much force can you push upward?
6. Using your forearm, with how much force can you push upward?

   Explain your results based on your knowledge of levers. Do the results of this experiment agree with your predictions?

EXPLORING ON YOUR OWN

- What other examples of muscles acting as levers can you find in your body? Are they all third-class levers?
- How many tools can you find that are third-class levers? What are they?

EXPERIMENT 8

THE LEVER AS A SENSITIVE BALANCE

You can build a balance that will weigh very small items using simple, inexpensive materials.

THINGS YOU WILL NEED

- **small machine screw**
- **plastic soda straw**
- **pin**
- **scissors**
- **2 identical glasses or cans**
- **graph paper**
- **laboratory balance**
- **clothespin**
- **file card**
- **pen or pencil**
- **sand**

1. To begin, push a small machine screw about halfway into one end of a plastic soda straw.
2. Use scissors to cut out a small piece from the top of the straw on the end opposite the machine screw. The cut out area will serve as a small balance pan.
3. Balance the straw and screw on your finger. Push a pin through the straw at the balance point. Be sure the pin, which will serve as the fulcrum, is just above the midpoint of the straw.
4. Place the fulcrum pin on a pair of glasses or cans. Turn the machine screw slowly until the beam

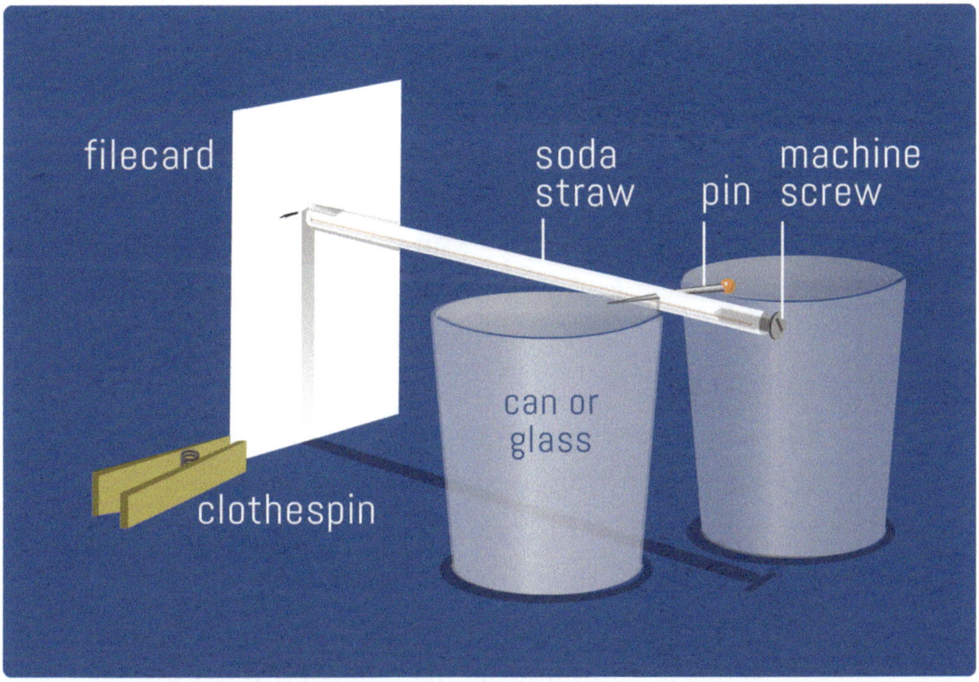

Figure 9. You can build a very sensitive balance that can weigh small masses. All you need are a few inexpensive items.

tilts upward at approximately 30 degrees (the precise degree of the angle is not important). (See Figure 9.)

5. To calibrate your balance, first find the mass, in grams, of a sheet of graph paper. Place the paper on a sensitive laboratory balance that can weigh fractions of a gram. (You could ask to borrow one from your school or use it in school and record the weight.)

6. Next, calculate the mass of one small square of the paper. For example, if the sheet weighs 3.0 g and contains 900 squares, each square must weigh 3.0 g ÷ 900, or 0.0033 g.
7. Use a clothespin to support a file card next to the balance pan. With a pen or pencil, mark the position of the balance pan you created on the card. Then place a known mass of paper squares on the pan. (In the example given, three squares would equal 0.01 g.)
8. Mark the new level of the pan on the card. Write the corresponding mass beside the mark. Do the same for several known masses.
9. What range of masses can you weigh with this balance? Can you weigh a grain of sand?

   What is good about this balance? What are its limitations? Can you build a better one?

CHAPTER TWO

OTHER SIMPLE MACHINES

So far we've done a number of experiments using levers but they are not the only simple machines. The wheel and axle, inclined plane, wedge, screw, and pulley are other examples of simple machines. Let's start with an experiment using the wheel and axle, which is similar in many ways to the lever.

EXPERIMENT 9

THE WHEEL AND AXLE

Wheel and axle machines are often used to lift heavy weights. You may ride atop a wheel-and-axle every day (your bicycle). You can use a bicycle wheel to experiment with this simple machine.

With a little imagination, you may be able to see that the wheel and axle acts like a circular lever.

THINGS YOU WILL NEED

- **bicycle**
- **tape**
- **string**
- **weight**
- **ruler**
- **meter stick or yardstick**
- **spring scale**

1. Turn a bicycle upside-down.
2. Tape one end of a short string to the top of the front tire. (See Figure 10.)
3. Tie one end of a longer string to the inner end of a spoke next to the front axle.
4. Wrap that string three or four times around the axle next to the spoke.
5. Attach a mass of known weight to the free end of the string (Figure 10).
6. Use a ruler to measure the diameter of the axle. Use a meter stick or yardstick to measure the radius of the wheel. Record your measurements.

   Based on your measurements, what is the theoretical mechanical advantage of this wheel and axle? (See Experiment 1 if you've forgotten about mechanical advantage.)
7. Using a spring scale, measure the force that has to be applied to the wheel to move the weight upward.

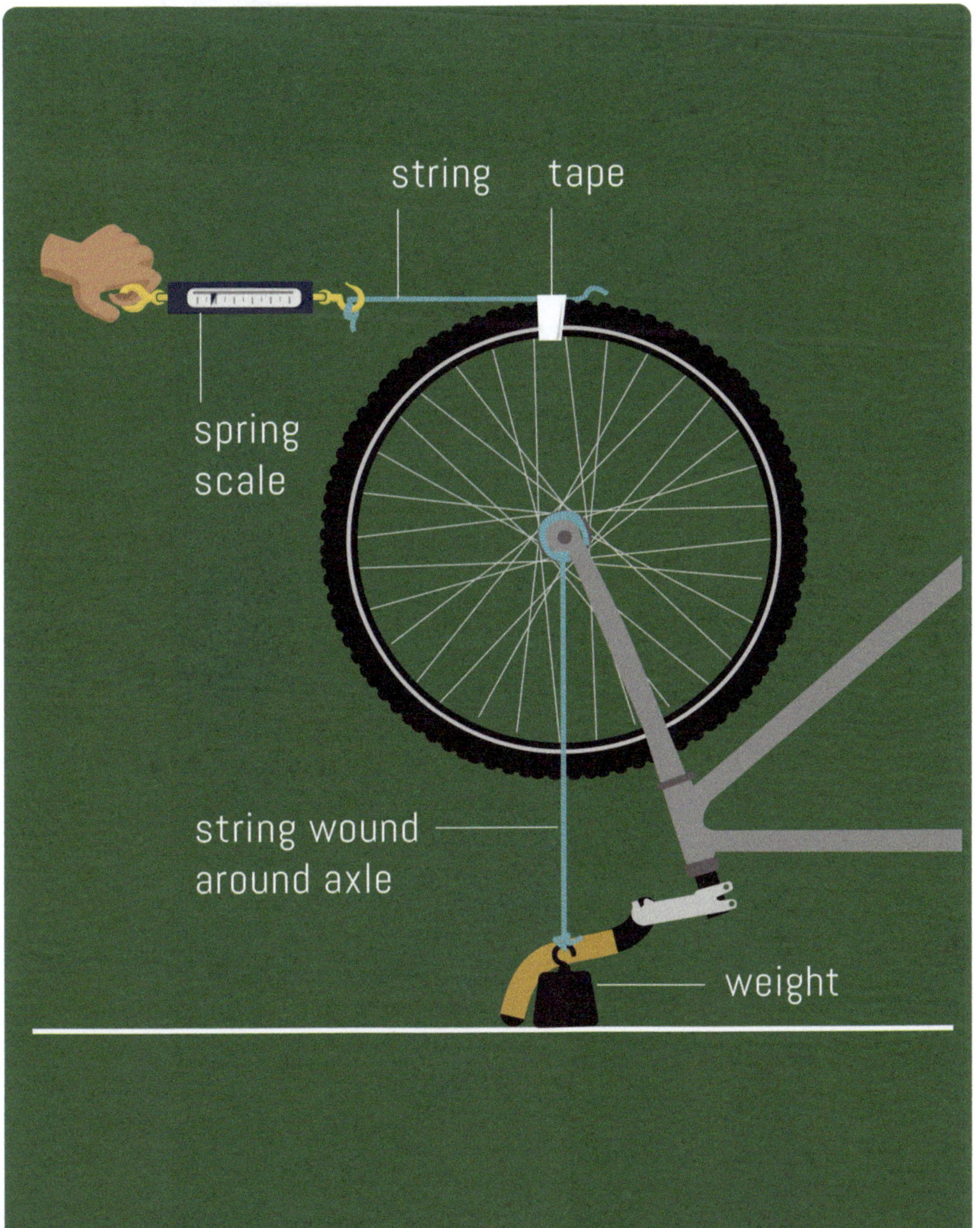

Figure 10. A bicycle wheel can serve as a wheel-and-axle machine. What mechanical advantage can it provide? How efficient is it?

What is the actual mechanical advantage of this machine? How much work would be needed to raise the weight from the ground to the axle?

8. Remove the weight. Wrap the string around the axle a few more times. When you reconnect the weight, it should be several inches off the floor.
9. Measure the height of the bottom of the weight from the floor. Then predict how high the weight will be lifted if you turn the wheel around once. Try it! Was your prediction correct?

How many times would the wheel have to be turned to lift the weight from the ground to the axle? How much work would you have to do? This is the work input—the work you would actually do to lift the weight using the wheel.

If *you* lifted the weight from the ground to the axle, how much work would you do? This is the work output–the work that has actually been accomplished.

Efficiency is defined as $\frac{\text{work output.}}{\text{work input}}$

What is the efficiency of this wheel and axle?

EXPERIMENT 10

THE INCLINED PLANE

The inclined plane is another simple machine designed to make work easier. You often see inclined planes as an alternative to stairs near building entrances. The inclined plane, or ramp, makes it possible for wheelchairs to access buildings.

THINGS YOU WILL NEED

- **tape**
- **a weight**
- **spring scale**
- **long board**
- **books**
- **meter stick, yardstick, or ruler**
- **toy truck**

Even though it may require more work, sometimes it makes sense to use a machine. The machine reduces the force needed to do a job even if requires more overall work (is less efficient). The following experiment will help you to see why.

1. Tape a mass that weighs about 500 g (1 lb) to a toy truck.
2. Use a spring scale to weigh the truck and its load, either together or separately. Record the total weight.
3. Use a long board and some books to build an inclined plane (Figure 11).

4. Measure and record the distance from the floor to the high end of the inclined plane.

   How much work would you do if you lifted the loaded truck from the floor straight up to the top of the incline? (Remember work = force × distance. See the section on Machines and Work for more information.)
5. Place the loaded truck at the low end of the inclined plane. What force is needed to pull the truck slowly up the inclined plane?

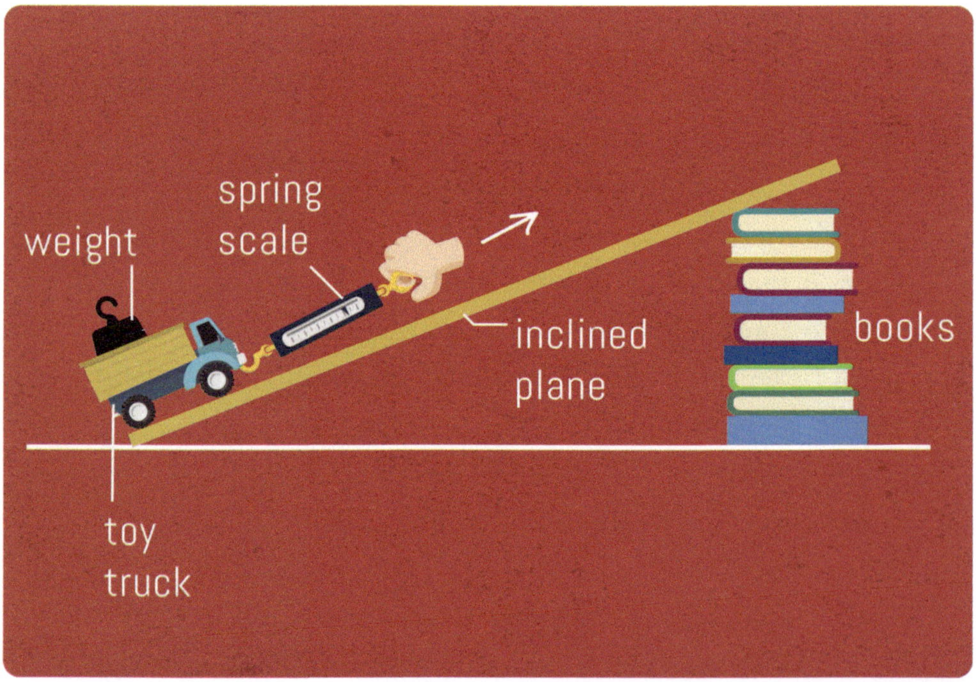

Figure 11. What force is needed to pull the toy truck and its load up the incline? How much work is required?

6. How much less force is needed to pull the truck along the incline than to lift it straight up? Measure and record the length of the inclined plane. How much work would be required to move the truck along the full length of the inclined plane? Why might this work be more than the work required to lift the truck straight up? Why might you use an inclined plane to raise a heavy load even if it involved more work?

EXPERIMENT 11

PULLEYS

Pulleys are used in places as diverse as farms, factories, or even your own garage. They are used to change the direction of a force or to reduce the force needed to move a heavy object. If you don't own any pulleys, you can use empty thread spools. To suspend the spool-pulley, put a wire through the hole in the

THINGS YOU WILL NEED

- **pulleys or spools**
- **hook or other means of support for pulley**
- **string**
- **object to lift (a weight or load)**
- **spring scale**
- **double pulleys (optional)**

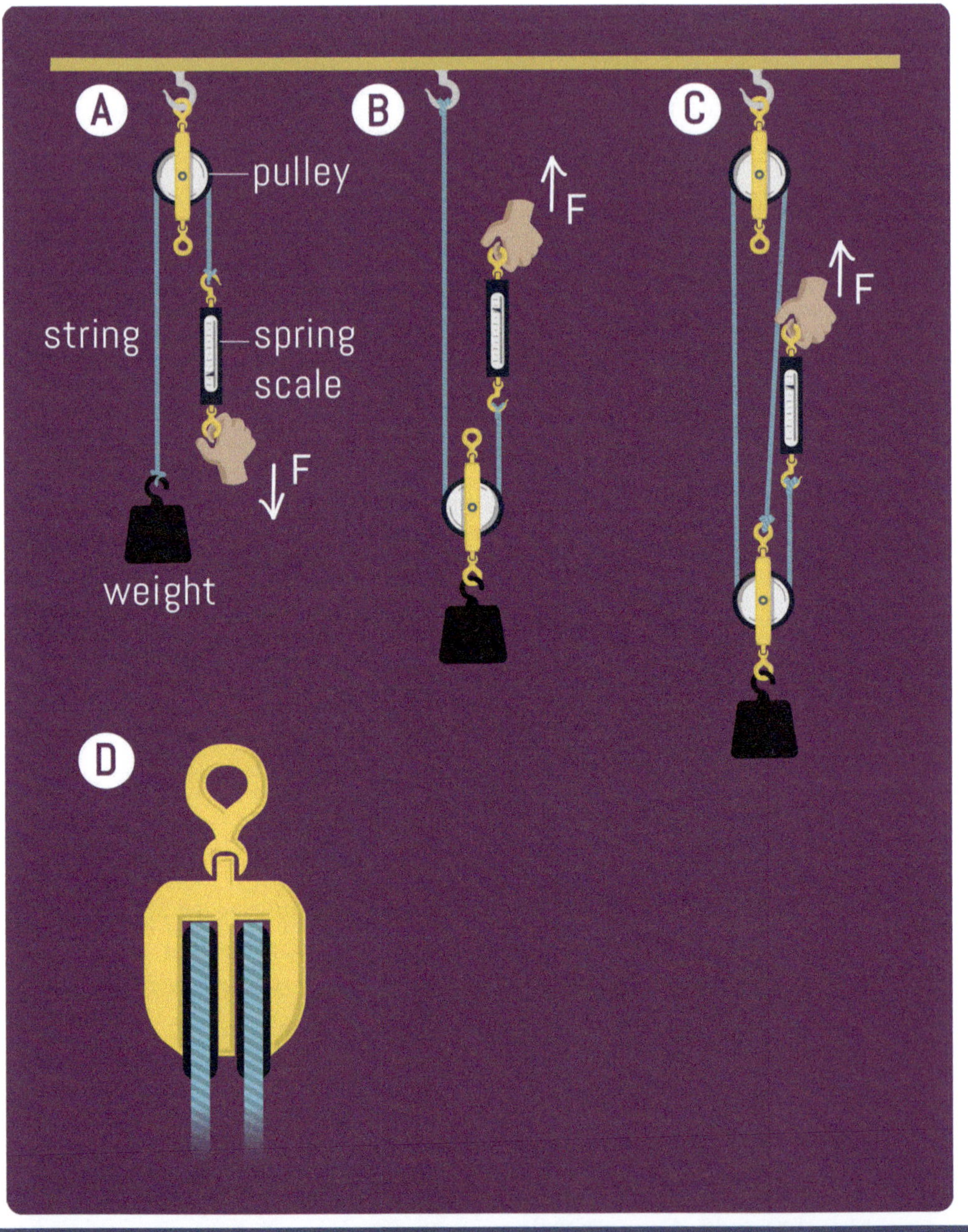

Figure 12. Compare the forces to lift a load using different pulley arrangements. a) A single fixed pulley and a downward force is used to lift the load. b) A single moveable pulley and an upward force is used to lift the load. c) Two pulleys (one fixed) and an upward force involving three strings are used to lift the load. d) A double pulley.

spool. The ends of the wire can be bent to make hooks so the pulley can be suspended (see Figure 12).

1. Attach a pulley to a hook or other means of support as shown in Figure 12a.
2. Tie a string to an object that can serve as the load or weight. Run the string over the pulley.
3. Lift the object using the pulley and a spring scale attached to the other end of the string.

   You may notice that this arrangement is similar to an equal-arm lever. How does the force you use to lift the object compare with the object's weight?

   Why would anyone use a single pulley to lift a weight?
4. Next, suspend the pulley using string and a hook (Figure 12b).
5. Attach a weight (load) to the pulley.
6. Lift the load using a spring scale. Measure the force needed to raise the load. What is the mechanical advantage of this pulley? Why was the force to lift the weight with this single pulley less than before? (Hint: How does the distance your force moves compare with the distance the load moves? Remember, work equals force times distance.)
7. If you have two pulleys, arrange them and the load as shown in Figure 12c. As you can see, three strings are now lifting the load. How does the force you apply now compare with the weight of the load?

If you have double pulleys (Figure 12d), measure the force to lift the load when four strings pull upward on the load.

EXPLORING ON YOUR OWN

Can you overcome the combined force of two people with a pulley system like the one in Figure 13? Use a sturdy rope or twine and see how many times you need to wrap it around the dowels before you can prevent two people from pulling the dowels apart.

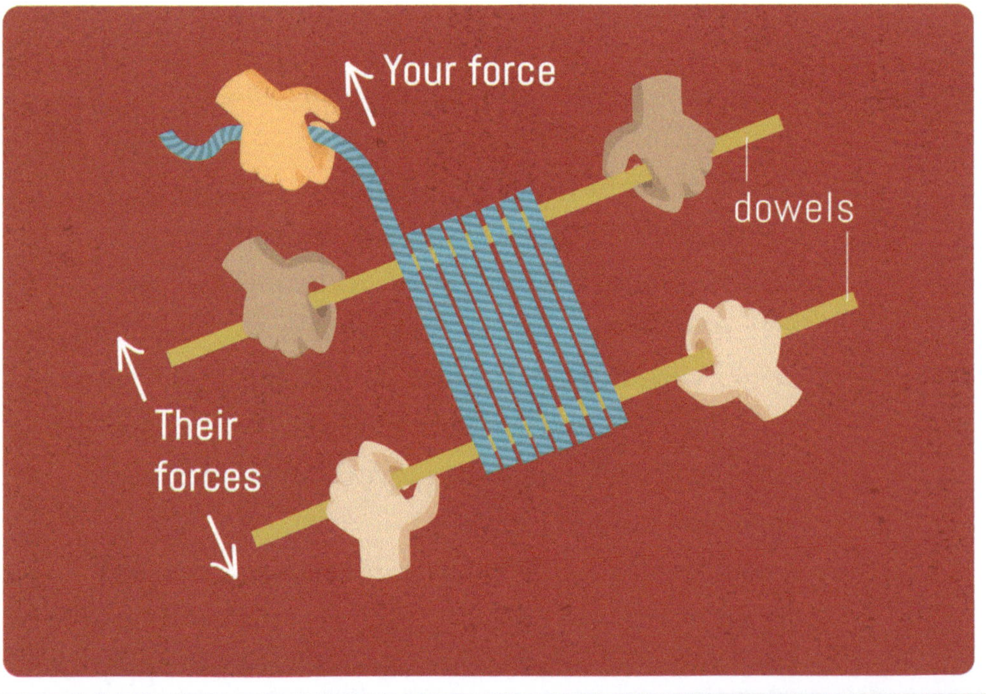

Figure 13. How many loops are needed to overcome the force of two people?

EXPERIMENT 12

THE WEDGE

THINGS YOU WILL NEED

- **3-inch x 5-inch file card**
- **ruler**
- **tape**
- **cardboard**

You can think of a wedge as two inclined planes with their bases together. It's a truly simple machine, but a very useful one. Wedges can be used to push things apart. Both authors have used wedges and a wedge on a handle—an ax— to split wood. You'll also find wedges used to keep doors open.

You can make a small wedge from a 3-inch × 5-inch file card.

1. Fold the file card in half, as shown in Figure 14.
2. Fold 1/2 inch of each end of the card toward each other as shown.
3. Tape these folded ends together. You now have a small wedge.
4. Use your wedge to lift a piece of cardboard. Slowly push the wedge under the cardboard. Push until you have raised the cardboard as high as possible.

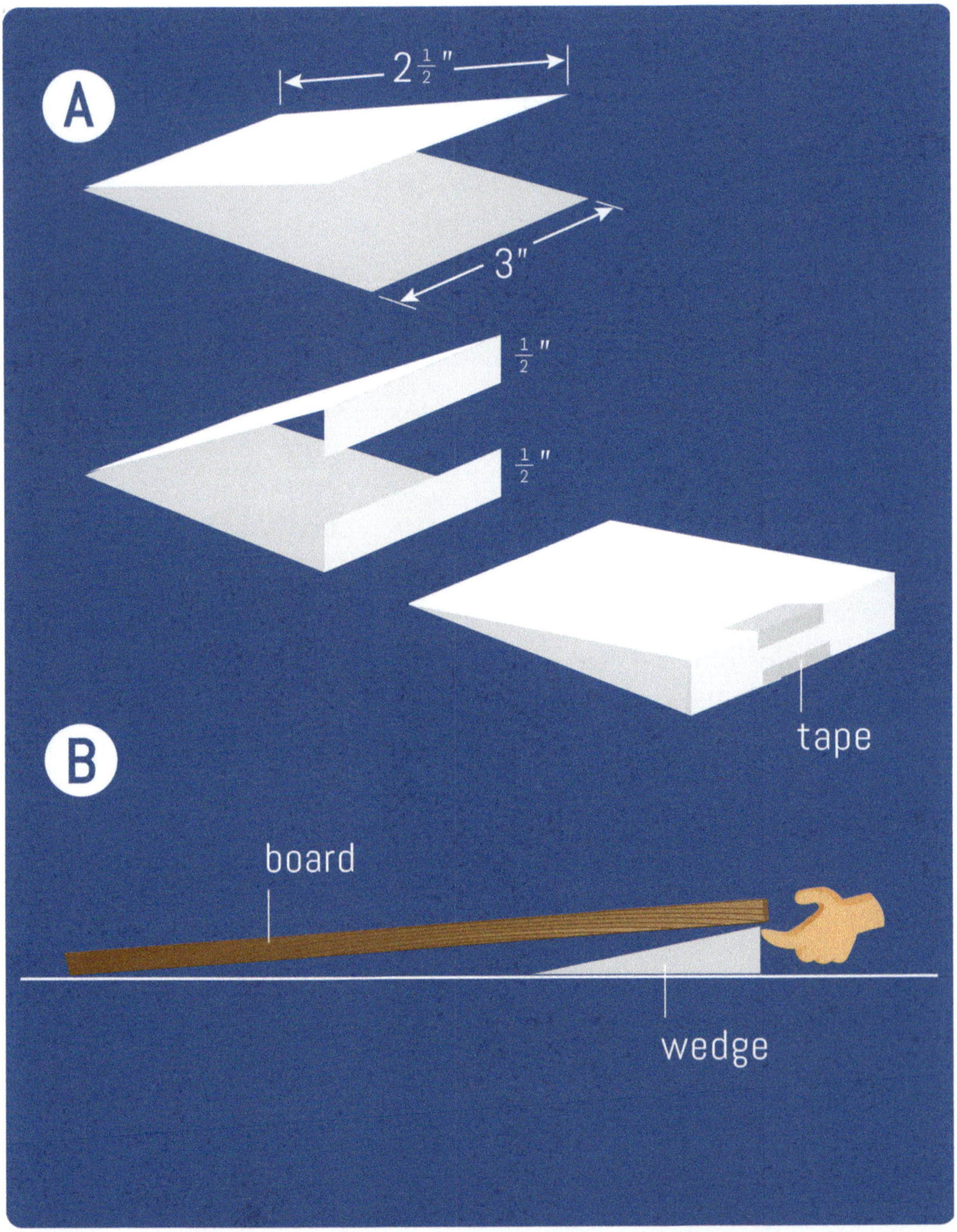

Figure 14. Make and use a simple wedge to lift a weight.

How far did the wedge move as it lifted the cardboard? How far upward did the end of the cardboard move? How did the force on the wedge compare with the force on the cardboard? How could you make your wedge stronger? How does a wedge make work easier? How many tools can you think of that are really wedges?

EXPERIMENT 13

THE SCREW OR BOLT

Screws and bolts are really inclined planes wound around a cylinder. To see that this is true, you can do this experiment.

THINGS YOU WILL NEED

- **paper**
- **ruler**
- **scissors**
- **pencil**
- **large, long bolt and nut**
- **wide washer that fits on bolt**
- **plastic bottle, such as an aspirin bottle with a neck narrower than the washer**
- **heavy object such as a brick or concrete block**
- **marker, such as an open paper clip**
- **wrench to turn the nut**

1. Cut out a paper triangle 28 cm (11 inches) long and 15 cm (6 inches) high (Figure 15a).
2. Starting with the wide end, wind the paper around a pencil

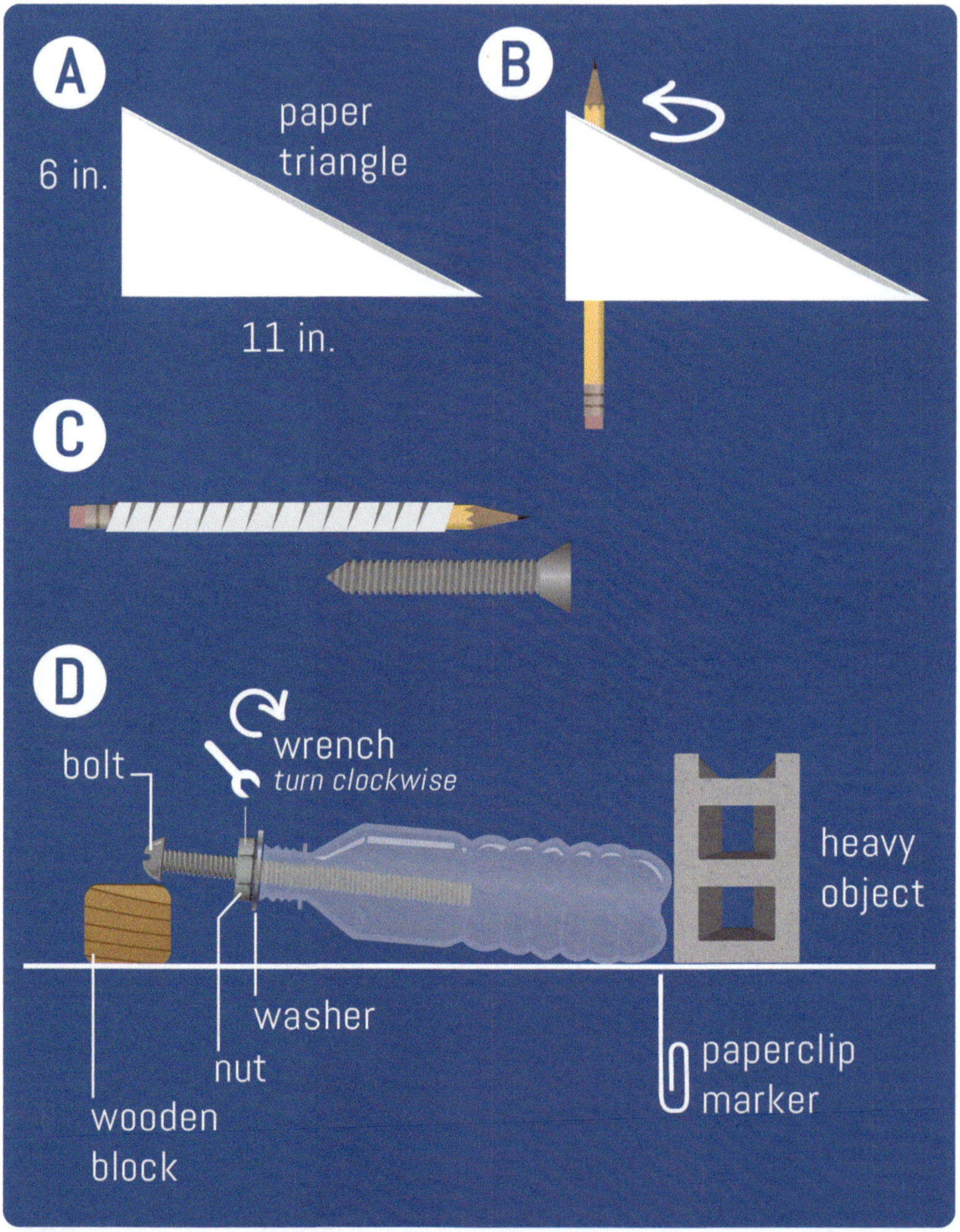

Figure 15. a) Cut a triangle 6 inches by 11 inches from a sheet of paper. b) Wind the triangle around a pencil. c) Notice that the pencil now looks like the threads on a screw or bolt. d) Use a bolt to move a heavy object.

(Figure 15b). The very thin inclined plane is now spiraled around the pencil.

3. Compare what you made with the threads on a bolt or screw (Figure 15c).
4. To see how screws or bolts make work easier, thread a nut on a large, long bolt. Add a wide washer.
5. Put the end of the bolt into a plastic bottle. Be sure the neck of the bottle is narrower than the washer. You will want the washer to push against the neck of the plastic bottle. (See Figure 15d.)
6. Place the bottom of the bottle against a heavy object such as a brick or a concrete block. Put a marker, such as an open paper clip, at the end of the heavy object. The marker will let you see how much the heavy object moves.
7. Put a wooden block under the head of the bolt. Then put your foot on the head of the bolt so it can't turn.
8. Use a wrench to turn the nut causing the washer to push on the bottle. The bottle will apply a force to the heavy object, causing it to move.

How many times must the nut turn to move the block one centimeter? Over how many screw threads does the nut move to do this?

It is easy to move the block by turning the nut. How hard is it to move the block by pushing it with your hand?

How is this machine a combination of simple machines?

CHAPTER THREE

THE FRICTION PHENOMENON

As explained in the previous chapter, friction reduces the mechanical advantage and efficiency of machines. However, as you will see, friction is essential to our everyday existence in other ways.

EXPERIMENT 14

WALKING FRICTION

If you have ever slipped on a patch of ice, you know that even a reduction in friction can make walking a challenge. If friction were to somehow disappear, walking would be impossible. You can see why by doing this experiment.

THINGS YOU WILL NEED

- **2 adults**
- **long, wide board**
- **a dozen wooden dowels about as long as the board's width**
- **smooth, level floor**

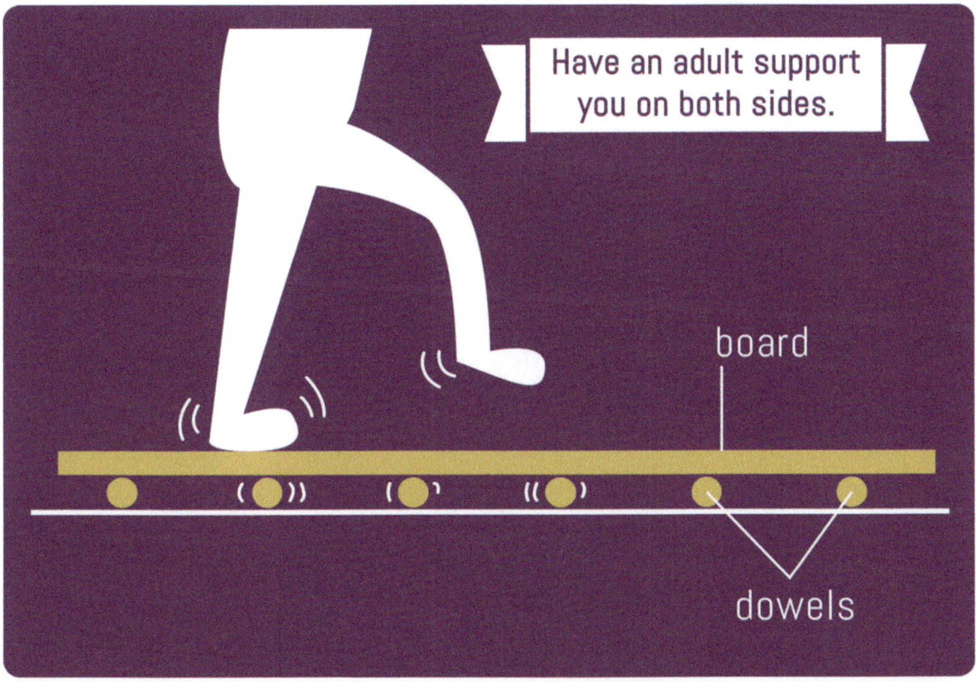

Figure 16. How does walking the plank help you understand why friction is needed to walk? (As you will learn later, it also illustrates Newton's third law of motion.)

1. Walk slowly along a smooth, level floor. As you walk, notice that you push back against the floor with one foot as you step forward with the other. It is your push backward against the floor that allows you to move forward. You are, in fact, pushing against the earth as the earth pushes back against you. What happens if you can't push against the earth?
2. Place about a dozen wooden dowels, parallel to one another, on a smooth, level floor. Leave a space of

about six inches between the dowels.

3. Place a long, wide board on the dowels.
4. With **two adults to hold on to you**, one on either side, carefully step onto the board (Figure 16).
5. Continue to hold onto the adults as you begin to walk along the board.

   Which way do you move? Which way does the board move?
6. Carefully get off the board while holding onto the two adults.

Walking on a board resting on rollers is like walking on wet ice. When you try to walk on such a slippery surface, it is nearly impossible. There is no friction between your feet and the surface. As a result, you can't push against the earth and, therefore, the earth can't push against you.

When you push against something, that something pushes back. It's Newton's third law of motion, which you'll learn more about in the next chapter.

In what other ways does friction play a role in our lives?

EXPERIMENT 15

MEASURING FRICTION

Friction is a force that always opposes motion. You can measure that force and see how it varies in different circumstances.

THINGS YOU WILL NEED

- four or more smooth wood blocks of the same size (You might ask an adult to cut them from a length of 2" x 4" lumber, and then you can smooth them with sandpaper.)
- large board, table, or counter
- sensitive spring scale or small weights, such as identical washers
- string
- pulley
- paper clips
- wide rubber bands
- felt pads
- thumbtacks
- aluminum foil, waxed paper, and plastic wrap (optional)
- Masonite board
- chipboard
- kitchen counter
- linoleum and other surfaces
- tape
- small wooden dowels or round pencils

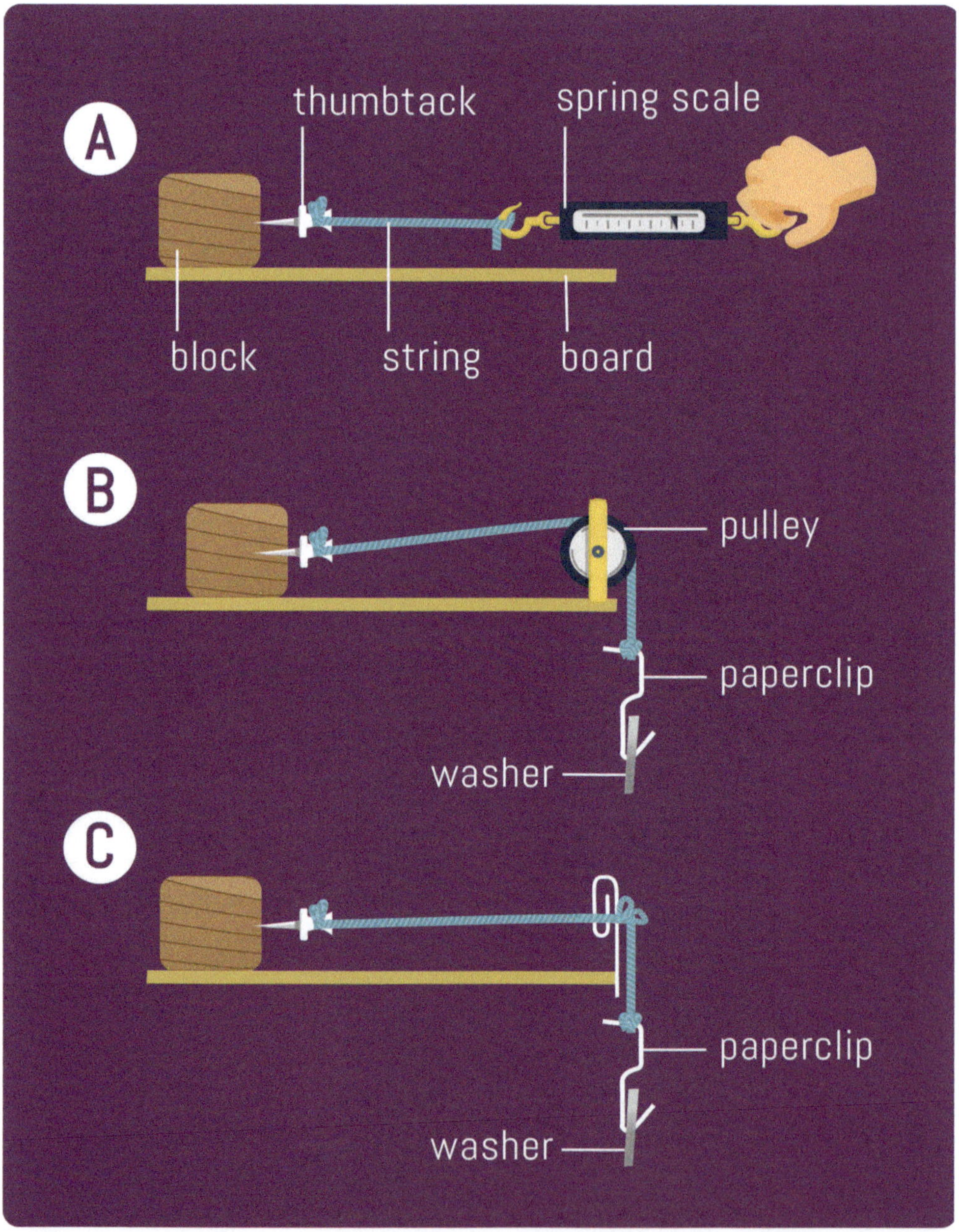

Figure 17. The frictional force on a block can be measured with a string and: a) a spring scale; b) a pulley and small weights; c) a bent paper clip and small weights.

1. Place a smooth wood block on a smooth level surface such as a board, a table, or a counter. Place a thumbtack into the board and tie a string to thumbtack. Attach string to a sensitive spring scale and pull the block, as shown in Figure 17a. Pull at a slow steady speed. The force you are using to pull the block equals the force of friction.
2. If you don't have a sensitive spring scale, you can use small weights, such as identical washers to pull on the block. (See Figure 17b.) A small pulley will allow you to add weights to a string attached to the block. A paper clip can be used to attach weights to the string. If you don't have a pulley, a bent paper clip can support the string as shown (Figure 17c). (If you want to know the force in grams or ounces, you can weigh the washers on a balance.)
3. Static friction is the frictional force between two surfaces at rest. Kinetic friction is the force when one surface is moving over another. Static friction is greater than kinetic friction. Therefore, it takes more force to make the block start to slide than to keep it sliding. If you are using weights to pull the block, tap the surface with your finger after adding a weight. It will help break the static friction.

HOW DOES THE KIND OF SURFACE AFFECT THE FRICTIONAL FORCE?

4. Prepare several blocks with different surfaces. Leave one block unchanged. Put wide rubber bands over a

second block, felt pads on a third, push thumbtacks into another. (The thumbtacks will go in easier if you use a second block to press them in.) You might also prepare surfaces using aluminum foil, waxed paper, or plastic wrap.

5. Compare the frictional force using these different surfaces on the blocks as they move at constant speed. On which surface is the friction greatest? On which is the friction least? List the surfaces in order of decreasing friction.
6. Pull the same blocks over a surface other than the board, table, or counter you have been using. You might use both sides of a Masonite board, a piece of chipboard, linoleum, or other available surfaces. Does the surface on which the blocks slide affect the force of friction? Does it affect the order of the blocks on the list you made?

WEIGHT, SURFACE AREA, AND FRICTION

7. Does weight affect friction? To find out, double the weight of a block by placing a second block on the first. Again, measure the force needed to make the two blocks move at a steady speed. How does the force required to move a stack of two blocks compare with the force needed for a single block?
8. Predict the force needed to pull a stack of three blocks along the same surface. Try it! Was your prediction correct?

9. To test the effect of surface area on friction, use tape to connect the sides of two blocks together like a "train." You already know the force needed to move two blocks when they are stacked. Now you can keep the weight the same but change the area on which there is friction. What have you done to the total surface area in contact with the board or table by making the two blocks into a train?
10. Measure the force needed to move the two-block train at a steady speed. How does the force compare with the force needed to move two blocks with half as much surface area?

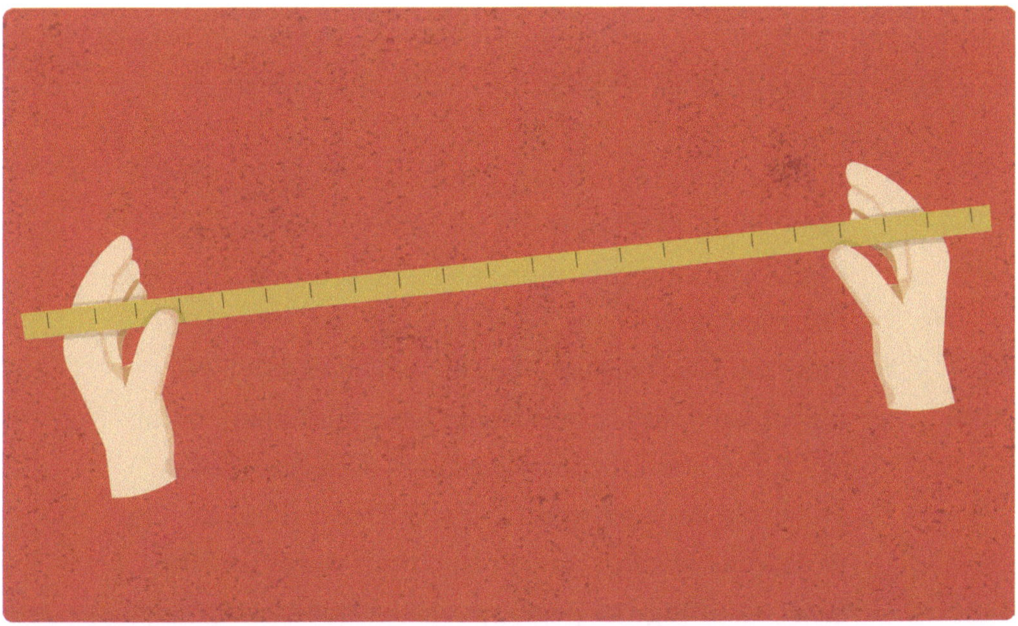

Figure 18. Rest a yardstick or meter stick on your outstretched hands. What happens as you slowly move your hands together? Where do your hands meet?

11. Repeat the experiment using three blocks. How does the force needed to move a three-block train compare with the force needed to move a three-block stack?

    What can you conclude about the effect of weight on friction? What can you conclude about the effect of surface area on friction?
12. Here's a simple experiment involving friction that may surprise you. You may find that center of mass is involved as well. Rest a meter stick or yardstick on your outstretched hands as shown in Figure 18. Your hands should be near the ends of the stick. Now, slowly bring your hands together. At what point under the stick do they meet? Can you explain why they meet there?

EXPLORING ON YOUR OWN

- If you use thumbtacks for the block's surface, what can you do to change the thumbtack surface area? Does doubling the thumbtack surface area affect the force needed to overcome friction?
- How can you change the surface area of contact for a rubber-band surface on a block? Does the amount of rubber surface affect the force needed to overcome friction?
- Take two large paperback books. Treat them as two decks of cards and shuffle their pages together. After shuffling the pages, push the books as closely together as possible. Now try to pull the books apart. How can you explain your inability to do so?

EXPERIMENT 16

FRICTION AND BEARINGS

THINGS YOU WILL NEED

- **2 full one-gallon cans (such as cans of paint)**
- **6 glass marbles of equal size**

As you found in Experiment 2, wheels can be used to reduce friction. Wheels, however, are usually connected to axles and there is friction when wheels turn on their axles. To reduce the friction, bearings are placed between the wheels and the axles. In this experiment, you'll see how bearings reduce friction.

1. Stack a full one-gallon can on top of a second identical can. Turn the top can on the bottom one and feel the force needed.
2. Remove the top can.
3. Place six identical glass marbles, which will act like ball bearings, along the rim of the lower can, separated as equally as possible.
4. Replace the upper can. Again feel the force needed to turn the top can. Have the bearings reduced friction?

CHAPTER FOUR

NEWTON'S LAWS OF MOTION

Sir Isaac Newton was arguably the greatest scientist of all time. He discovered that sunlight consists of many colors by passing the sun's light through a prism, invented the mathematics we call calculus, developed the reflecting telescope and, building on Galileo's work, developed the three laws of motion and the universal law of gravitation.

The three laws of motion are essential to an understanding of engineering and, indeed, a vast amount of science. In this chapter, you'll investigate and experiment with these three laws.

EXPERIMENT 17

NEWTON'S FIRST LAW OF MOTION

Often called the law of inertia, the first law of motion has two parts. The first part states that a body at rest remains at rest unless acted upon by an outside force. No one objected to this part of the law. The second part states that a body in motion remains in motion at a constant velocity unless acted on by an outside force.

THINGS YOU WILL NEED

- **small nail**
- **hammer**
- **metal jar cap**
- **glue**
- **empty spool of thread**
- **balloon**
- **smooth, level surface such as a countertop**
- **small block**

At the time Newton published his laws, most people believed that a moving object required a force to ***keep it*** in motion. Newton's vivid imagination and depth of perception led him to a different conclusion. He reasoned that in the absence of a force an object would continue to move with a steady velocity forever. He realized that most moving objects eventually stop because friction, a force, opposes their motion.

We can't eliminate friction, but it can be substantially reduced. Then you can see what moving at a constant velocity without a force looks like, at least for a short period.

1. Using a small nail and a hammer, punch a single hole through the center of the top of a metal jar cap (Figure 19a).
2. Glue an empty spool to the bottom of the jar cap (Figure 19b). Be sure the holes in the spool and jar cap align.

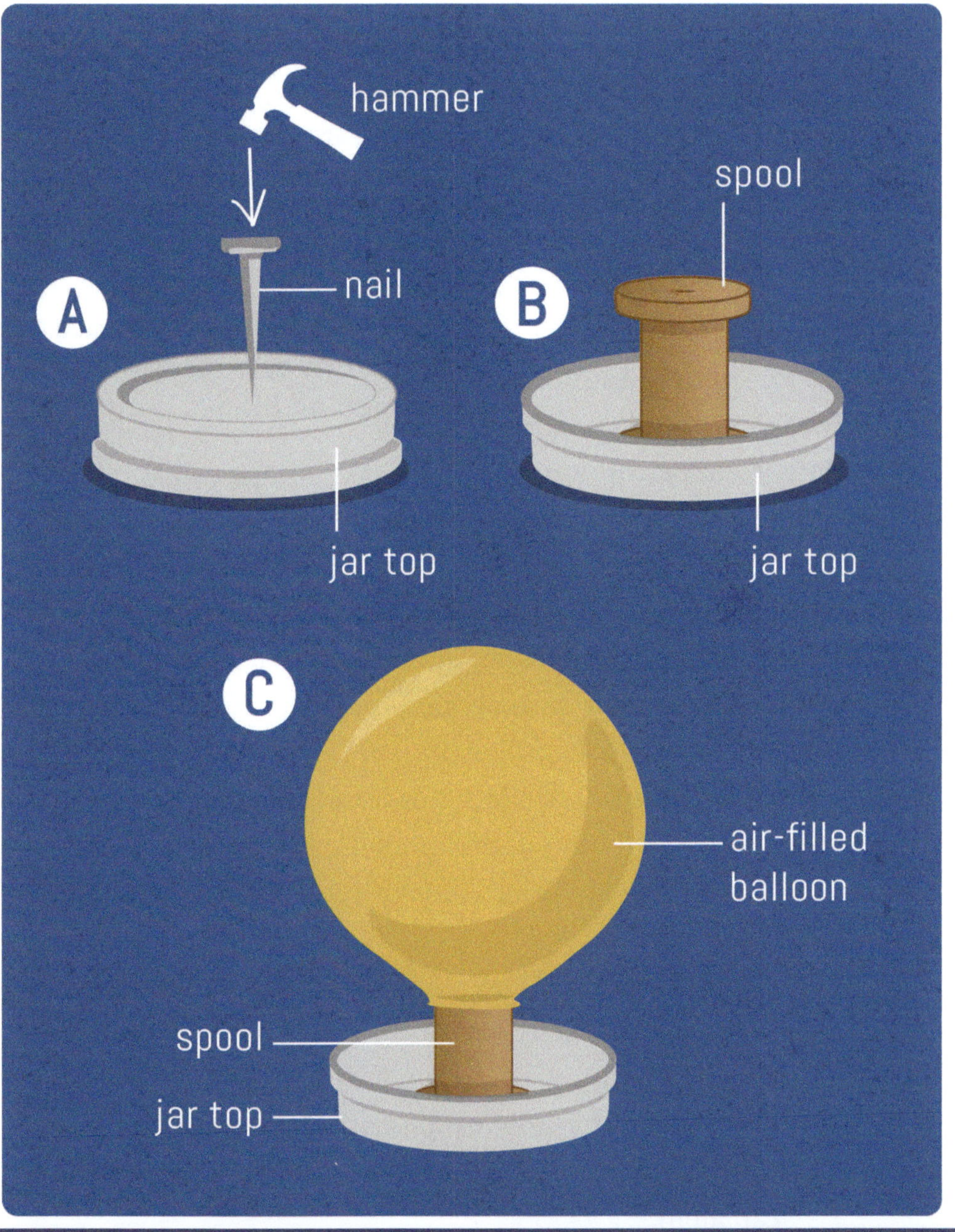

Figure 19. a) Punch a small hole in the top of side of a metal jar top. b) Glue an empty spool to the bottom side of the jar top. Be sure the holes line up. c) Attach an air-filled balloon to the spool. You now have an "air car." Give it a small push so it moves slowly across a smooth level surface.

3. When the glue has dried, pull the neck of an inflated balloon over the top of the spool (Figure 19c). Hold your finger or a block against the hole in the jar cap to keep the air from escaping.
4. Place this "air car" on a very smooth, level surface such as a countertop. Quickly remove your finger or the block and give the air car a little push. Watch it glide along with no further help from you. Does it appear to move at a constant speed? What makes it stop?
5. To see another way that a body in motion remains in motion at a constant velocity try this:

   Walk along an uncarpeted hallway or some other long hard-surfaced floor carrying a tennis ball. As you walk, drop the ball. When the ball bounces do you have to stop to catch it, or can you keep walking and catch it? That is, does its horizontal velocity remain constant?

   What happens if you stop walking a moment after you drop the ball? How does this experiment illustrate Newton's first law?
6. You can come even closer to observing the kind of ongoing motion Newton imagined. Watch a puck slide across the surface of a level air-hockey table. Give the puck a slight push and watch it continue to move. What do you notice about its speed? Its direction of motion? When does it change direction? How can you explain its change in direction?

NEWTON'S SECOND LAW OF MOTION

Newton's second law states that when a force is applied to a mass, the mass will accelerate in the direction of the force. The acceleration, a, will equal the ratio of the force, F, to the mass, m, or

$$a = F/m.$$

To fully understand Newton's second law, you need to distinguish between mass and weight. You also need to understand what is meant by acceleration and how it is measured.

MASS AND WEIGHT

People often confuse mass and weight. Mass is the amount of matter in an object. It can be determined using an equal arm balance. Weight is a measure of the force exerted on a mass by gravity. One way to understand the difference between mass and weight is to think about taking a trip to the moon.

Suppose that on earth your mass, as measured on a big equal arm balance, is 50 kilograms (kg). You sit on the balance's left pan; 50 kilograms is placed on the right pan and the balance beam is level.

Your weight, as determined by standing on a bathroom scale would be 490 newtons or 110 pounds. Your weight is the force with which Earth's gravity pulls you toward its center. (A newton is the force needed to move one kilogram with an acceleration of one meter per second per second [m/s^2]).

When you reach the moon, you find that your mass, as determined on an equal arm balance, is still 50 kg. There is no more or less of you. You are still the same amount of matter. However, when you step on a bathroom scale, your weight will be only 81 newtons or 18 pounds. The moon's gravity is only one-sixth as strong as earth's. It pulls on you with one-sixth as much force. So mass is independent of gravitational force, while weight depends on gravitational force.

The moon's gravity is less than Earth's because the moon has less mass than Earth. But it also has a smaller radius. Newton showed that the gravitational force at the surface of a planet depends on the planet's mass and its radius. The gravitational force is proportional to the planet's mass, but it is *inversely* proportional to the square of its radius. That is:

$$\text{Force} = \text{a constant} \times \frac{\text{mass of planet}}{\text{radius of planet} \times \text{radius of planet}} = \frac{\text{mass of planet}}{(\text{radius of planet})^2}$$

Now the moon's mass is only 0.0123 times the mass of Earth; its radius is 0.27 times that of Earth. Thus its gravity as compared to Earth's is:

$$\frac{0.0123}{0.27 \times 0.27} = \frac{0.0123}{0.0729} = 0.169\text{, or about } 1/6$$

Newton's second law applies only to the net force, the force that is greater than the force of friction or any other restraining force. The rule that acceleration is proportional to force means that doubling the net force will double the acceleration, tripling the net force will triple the acceleration, and so on. That acceleration and mass are inversely proportional means that, given the same force, doubling the mass will halve the acceleration, tripling the mass will reduce the acceleration to one-third, and so on.

The mass of an object can be determined on an equal-arm balance. Mass is usually measured in grams (g) or kilograms (kg). Weight is measured in newtons or pounds (more about that later).

ACCELERATION

Acceleration is the rate at which velocity changes. Mathematically speaking,

$$a = \Delta v / \Delta t.$$

The equation states that acceleration, a, equals the change in velocity, Δv, divided by the change in time, Δt. (The symbol Δ means "change in.")

Notice that acceleration is a change in velocity divided by a change in time, not a change in speed divided by time. The reason is that both velocity and acceleration have a direction as well as a magnitude (size). Speed does not have a direction.

Here's an example to show how acceleration is calculated.

What is the acceleration of a car that starts at rest and reaches a velocity of 60 mph south in 12 seconds? Note that a velocity of 60 mph is equal to 88 feet/second.

$$a = \Delta v / \Delta t = (88 \text{ ft/s} - 0 \text{ ft/s})/12 \text{ s} = 7.33 \text{ ft/s/s, or } 7.33 \text{ ft/s}^2.$$

You can detect acceleration by building a simple accelerometer. As an engineer, you might be asked to build a more sophisticated one that would actually measure the rate of velocity change.

EXPERIMENT 18

BUILDING AND TESTING ACCELEROMETERS

An accelerometer is a device that will indicate acceleration and its direction. In this experiment you will build two different accelerometers. Then you can use them to detect acceleration. The results may surprise you!

THINGS YOU WILL NEED

- thread
- T-pin or large needle
- tape
- clear plastic jar with screw-on cap
- cork or other light material such as Styrofoam
- vial or test tube and cork to fit opening
- small piece of soap
- level table or counter

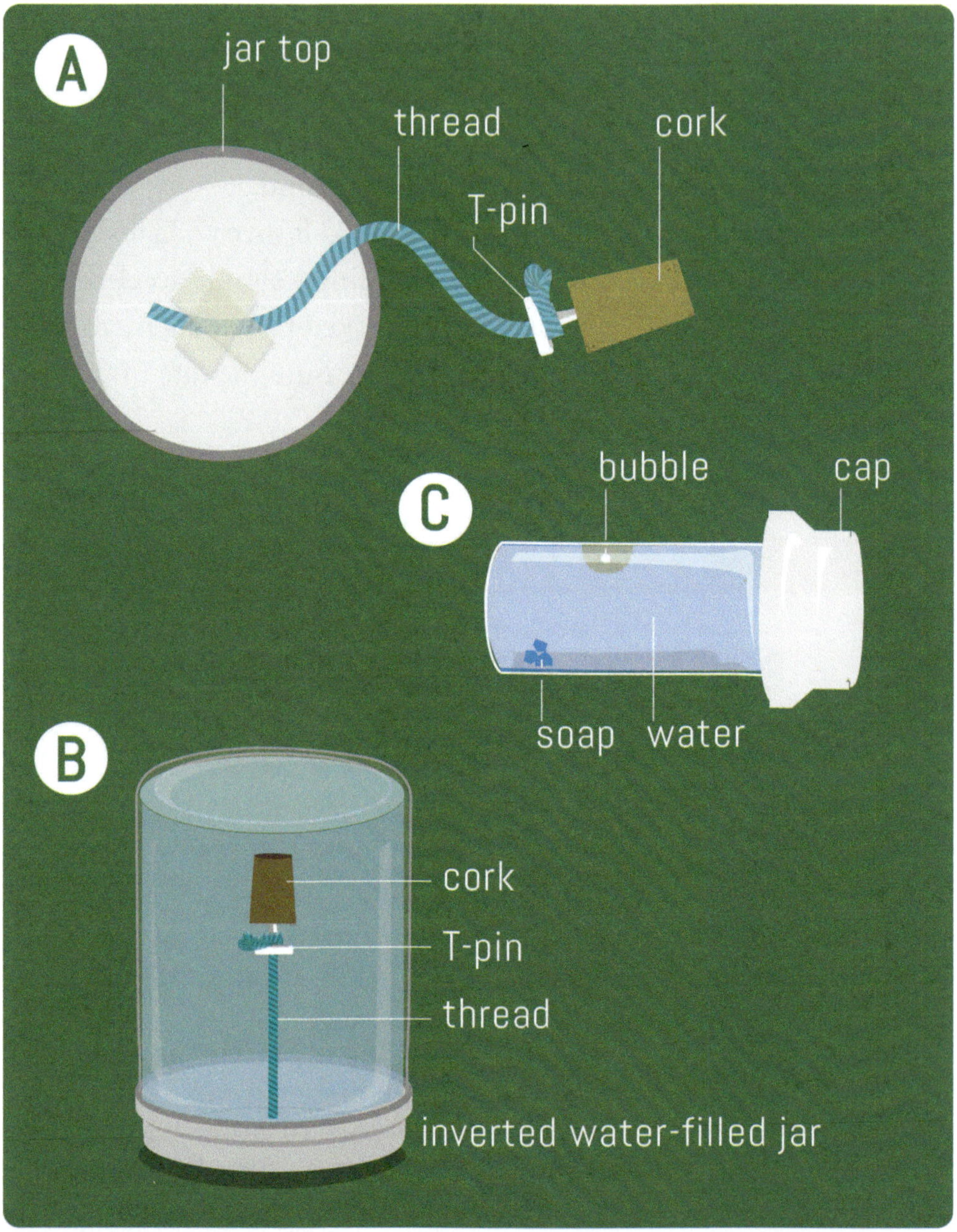

Figure 20. Two accelerometers you can build are shown here. a) The cap assembly for the jar accelerometer. b) The assembled jar accelerometer. c) A vial or test tube accelerometer uses a bubble to indicate acceleration.

1. Insert a T-pin (or large needle) into a cork or a piece of Styrofoam. (See Figure 20a).
2. Tie one end of a length of thread to the T-pin. Tape the other end of the thread securely to the inside of a screw-on cap of a clear plastic jar (Figure 20a). Make sure the thread is not so long that the cork will rub against the bottom of the jar when the accelerometer is assembled and inverted.
3. Fill the jar with water, screw on the cap assembly, and invert the jar. (Figure 20b)
4. You can also make a vial or test tube accelerometer. Fill the vial or tube with water leaving just enough space for a small bubble of air. Add a tiny piece of soap. The soap will prevent the bubble from sticking to the vial's surface. Cap the vial, or cork the test tube, and lay it on its side (Figure 20c).
5. To see how these instruments respond to accelerated motion, place them on a level table or counter.
6. Pull each one so that it accelerates. Notice that the cork or bubble always moves in the direction of the acceleration, which is also the direction of the force. When you start from rest and pull the accelerometer forward, the cork or bubble moves forward. How can you make the bubble or cork move just a little bit? How can you make it move a lot?
7. When the accelerometer slows and finally stops, the force (usually friction) opposes the motion. The

acceleration is negative (deceleration) because the velocity gets smaller. The cork or bubble moves the other way, opposite the motion, but, as always, in the direction of the force.

8. Take a walk carrying your accelerometer as you walk. Do you accelerate and decelerate while walking?
9. Hold the accelerometer at arm's length and turn around several times. What is the direction of the acceleration?
10. Take the accelerometer on an automobile or bus ride. In what direction is the acceleration when you go around a curve? (Note: there's nothing wrong with the accelerometer. When anything moves in a circle, the acceleration is inward toward the center of the circle. So is the force.)
11. Save the accelerometers you have built. You will use them in some later experiments in this book.

EXPERIMENT 19

THE ACCELERATION OF A FALLING OBJECT

Every mass on Earth is pulled toward Earth's center with a force that is proportional to its mass. As a result, the acceleration of all falling bodies is the same if there is no resistance to motion, such as the resistance of the air.

THINGS YOU WILL NEED

- **large rock and a smaller rock or baseball and tennis ball**
- **solid surface such as pavement or hard ground**
- **small sheet of paper**
- **book**

1. To see that all things fall with the same acceleration, hold a large rock in one hand and a smaller rock in the other hand. You could also use a baseball and a tennis ball.
2. Hold both rocks or balls in front of you at the same height above a solid surface such as pavement or hard ground.
3. Release both rocks or balls at the same time. Did both objects reach the ground at the same time?
4. Place a small sheet of paper on a book. Be sure the paper's area is smaller than the book's. Drop the book. Did paper and book fall together?
5. Hold the book with one hand and the paper with the other hand. Drop both at the same time. Did they fall together this time?

As you saw, the paper fell more slowly than the book. Air does resist the motion of objects. Light objects fall with less acceleration than heavy ones. But in a vacuum (where there is no air resistance) all objects fall with the same acceleration. If you search on the Internet for "hammer and feather drop on the moon" you should find a film of an astronaut dropping a feather and hammer on the moon. The feather falls with the same acceleration as the hammer because there is no air on the surface of the moon. The two objects were falling in a vacuum.

6. Figure 21 shows a scaled drawing of a portion of a tape that was attached to a falling mass. As the mass fell, it pulled the tape through a spark timer. The timer produced a spark every one-tenth of a second. Each spark made a hole in the paper.

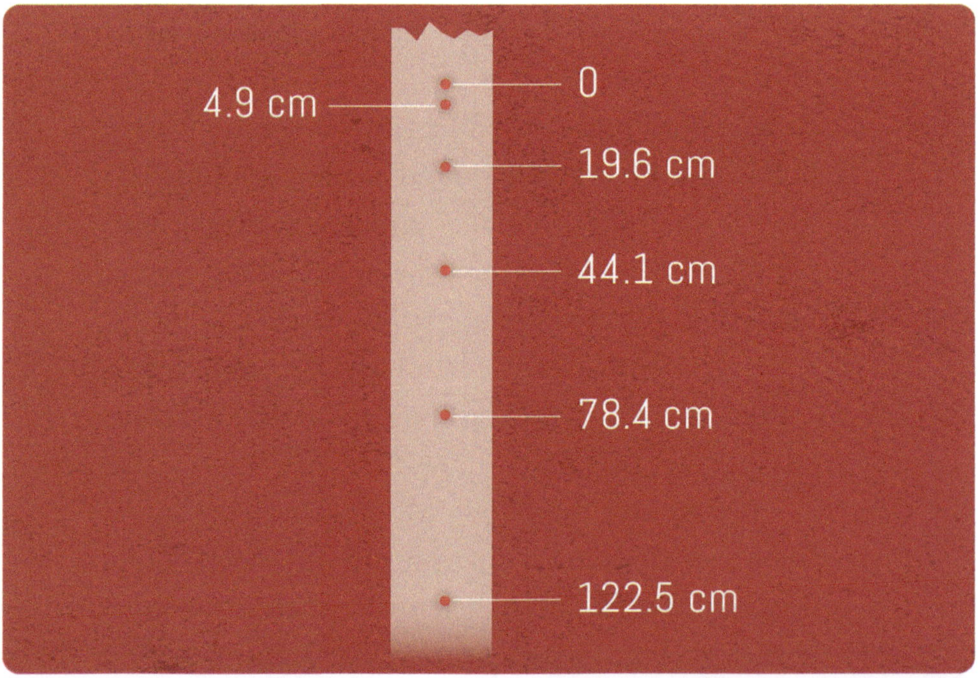

Figure 21. This is a scaled drawing of a tape that was pulled through a spark timer by a heavy falling mass. The timer produced a spark every 0.1 second. You can see from the separation of the holes burned through the tape by the sparks that the mass was accelerating as it fell. Use the data on the tape to calculate the acceleration (answer at the end of book).

7. The actual distances that the mass fell between successive sparks are given by successive holes on the tape as shown in the drawing. Use that information to find the acceleration of the falling mass. Remember:

$$a = \Delta v / \Delta t.*$$

* Answer can be found at the end of the book on page 117.

EXPERIMENT 20

TESTING NEWTON'S SECOND LAW OF MOTION

In his second law, Newton wrote that a mass will accelerate at a rate equal to the net force acting on it divided by the mass, or

$a = F/m$ or, in terms of the net force, $F = ma$.

In this experiment, you can test the law in a semi-quantitative way.

THINGS YOU WILL NEED

- **child's wagon**
- **heavy weights, such as concrete blocks, pails of sand, or other heavy object that can be duplicated**
- **smooth, level surface**
- **spring scale: 0–2000 gram (0–20 newton)**

1. Place a weight in a child's wagon. You might use a concrete block, a pail of sand, or some other heavy object. Be sure you have more than one heavy object.
2. Attach one of the accelerometers you built in Experiment 18 to the wagon.
3. Use a spring scale to pull the wagon along a smooth, level surface at a slow, constant speed. The spring scale allows you to measure the force pulling the wagon.

   What is the reading on the spring scale when the wagon moves at a steady speed? What does the accelerometer indicate? What is the frictional force between the wagon's wheels and the surface it is moving on? (Remember Experiment 15?)
4. What do you predict will happen if the force you apply to the wagon is less than the frictional force? Try it. Was your prediction correct?
5. What do you predict will happen when the force you use to pull the wagon is greater than the frictional force? To check your prediction, use the spring scale to pull the wagon with a force twice as large as the frictional force. Keep the spring stretched to that force as you pull the wagon along the smooth, level surface. What happens to the wagon's velocity as you pull it with this constant force? What does the accelerometer indicate? Was your prediction correct?
6. What will happen if you apply a force three times as big as the frictional force? Try it! What does the accelerometer indicate?

7. Next, increase the weight in the wagon by adding a second concrete block, pail of sand, or whatever you are using as weights. Measure the force needed to move the wagon along at a steady speed. Does weight affect the friction between the wagon's wheels and the surface?
8. Now pull on this heavier wagon with the same ***net force*** you applied to the lighter wagon. Remember, the net force is the total force minus the force of friction. For example, if you pulled on the wagon with a force of 200 grams (2.0 newtons) greater than the force of friction when you had one unit of weight in the wagon, do the same now that there are two units of weight in the wagon. That is, pull with a force 2.0 newtons greater than the frictional force on the wagon. You want the net force—the total force applied minus the frictional force—to be the same as it was with one unit of weight in the wagon.

Does the added weight of the wagon affect the rate at which the wagon's velocity increases under the same force? If it does, how?

You have seen that the wagon accelerates (increases its speed) when you apply a force greater than the force of friction that opposes its motion. You have seen, too, that the acceleration is greater when the force is greater and smaller when the mass is increased.

NEWTON'S THIRD LAW OF MOTION

According to Newton's third law: For every action there is always an equal and opposite reaction.

This law might be called the "push, push-back law." What it means is that if you push something or someone in one direction, that person or thing will push back on you with an equal force in the opposite direction. When you stand on a floor, you push *down* on the floor. The floor pushes *up* on you with an equal force.

EXPERIMENT 21

TESTING NEWTON'S THIRD LAW OF MOTION

You unknowingly tested Newton's third law when you did Experiment 14 to show that walking requires friction. Your foot pushed backward on the board; the board pushed forward on you. However, the board probably moved back faster than you moved forward because you had more mass than the board. When you walk along the ground, you push against the earth. The earth pushes back and you move forward. We don't see the earth move because its mass is far bigger than yours. The earth's mass is approximately 6×10^{24} kg or 6 trillion trillion kilograms.

THINGS YOU WILL NEED

- a partner
- ice or roller skates
- ice or smooth level surface
- oblong-shaped balloon
- twist ties
- string
- soda straw
- tape
- glass of water (1 or 2)
- balance and balance pan
- weight
- clay
- sharp pencil
- Styrofoam cup
- scissors
- two flexible drinking straws
- thread
- water
- sink

1. Both you and a partner should put on ice skates or roller skates.
2. Stand close together facing each other on ice (if using ice skates) or on a smooth level surface (if using roller skates).
3. When you are both ready, give your partner a small push. What happens?
4. Next, have your partner push you. What happens?
5. If possible, repeat the experiment with someone much heavier than you. What happens?
6. Again, if possible, repeat the experiment with someone who has less mass than you. What happens?

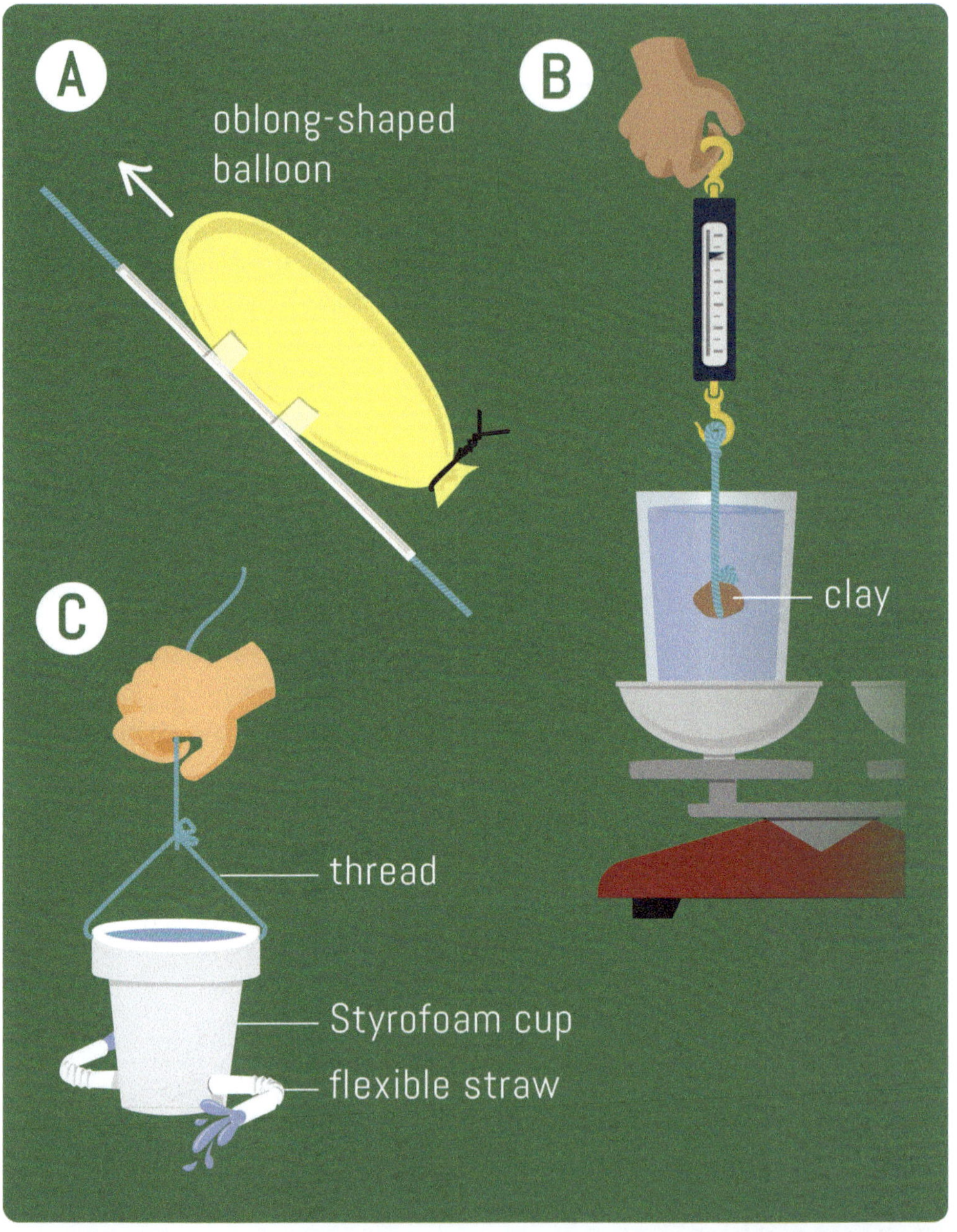

Figure 22. The drawings show some other ways of testing Newton's third law of motion.

OTHER TESTS OF NEWTON'S THIRD LAW

7. Blow up an oblong-shaped balloon. Seal the balloon's neck with a twist tie.
8. Tie one end of a long string to a high point in a room. Run the other end of the string through a soda straw.
9. Tape the straw to the balloon as shown in Figure 22a.
10. Have a partner hold the free end of the string taut as you remove the twist tie and release the balloon. What happens? How does this experiment illustrate Newton's third law?
11. Place a glass of water on a balance pan. Depending on the type of balance, balance the glass of water with weights, another glass of water, or, if it is an electronic balance, simply record the weight.
12. Attach a large ball of clay to one end of a string. Attach the other end to a spring balance. Predict what will happen to the weight of the clay and to the weight of the glass of water when you lower the clay into the water as shown in Figure 22b.

    Were you right? Did the clay push on the water? Did the water push on the clay? How does this experiment illustrate Newton's third law?
13. Using a sharp pencil, make two small holes near the bottom and on opposite sides of a Styrofoam cup.
14. With scissors, cut the ends off two flexible drinking straws.

15. Push one end of the flexible straw ends through the holes in the cup. Flex the straws as shown in Figure 22c.
16. Next, make two small holes on opposite sides near the top of the cup.
17. Run a piece of thread through both holes. Tie the ends to make a loop. Then tie a second piece of thread to the loop.
18. Hold the cup over a sink and fill the cup with water. Hold the end of the support thread as shown in Figure 22c.
19. Watch the water "jet" out from the straws. What happens to the cup? How does this experiment illustrate Newton's third law?
20. After the cup has emptied, turn one of the straw jets around so that it points in the opposite direction. Predict what will happen when you repeat the experiment. Were you right?
21. How does a rocket lifting off illustrate newton's third law?

EXPLORING ON YOUR OWN

- Devise other experiments to test Newton's third law of motion.
- If Earth and sun attract each other with equal and opposite forces due to gravity, why don't Earth and sun come together? (Hint: what did you find the direction of acceleration to be when an object moves in a circle?)

CHAPTER FIVE

GALILEO AND HOOKE, TWO OF NEWTON'S PRECURSORS

Newton reportedly once said, "If I have seen further than other men, it is because I stood on the shoulders of giants." Two of the giants Newton was referring to were Galileo Galilei and Robert Hooke. You'll meet both men and their work in this chapter.

EXPERIMENT 22

ACCELERATION DUE TO GRAVITY

Galileo was an Italian scientist born in 1564, long before spark timers were invented. Nevertheless, he did a number of experiments to measure the acceleration caused by gravity. Using Figure 21, you found the acceleration of a falling object. Galileo had no way to carry out such an experiment.

You also took two objects with different masses, such as a baseball and a tennis ball, held them the same height above the floor and released them simultaneously. Did they fall

THINGS YOU WILL NEED

- **straight, rigid, 3 meter (10 ft) section of aluminum or steel angle (V-shaped length of metal can be obtained from a hardware store)**
- **wood blocks or books**
- **marker**
- **hard rubber or large steel ball**
- **stopwatch**
- **pencil**
- **paper or notebook**
- **calculator**
- **graph paper**
- **string**
- **tape**
- **5 large marbles**

together striking the floor at the same time?

Galileo performed a similar experiment to disprove an ancient theory. The theory claimed an object twice as heavy would fall twice as fast. According to legend, Galileo dropped two cannonballs, one ten times heavier than the other from the Leaning Tower of Pisa. They both struck the ground at very nearly the same time.

Galileo believed objects accelerate as they fall. However, he had no way to measure the short time intervals needed to find the change in speed of falling objects. Therefore, he ***diluted*** gravity. He let a ball roll down an inclined plane. It was still gravity that pulled the ball down the incline. But, at a small angle, the ball rolled so slowly that he could measure its acceleration. He clearly demonstrated that the acceleration due to gravity was constant no matter the mass of an object. You can perform a similar experiment.

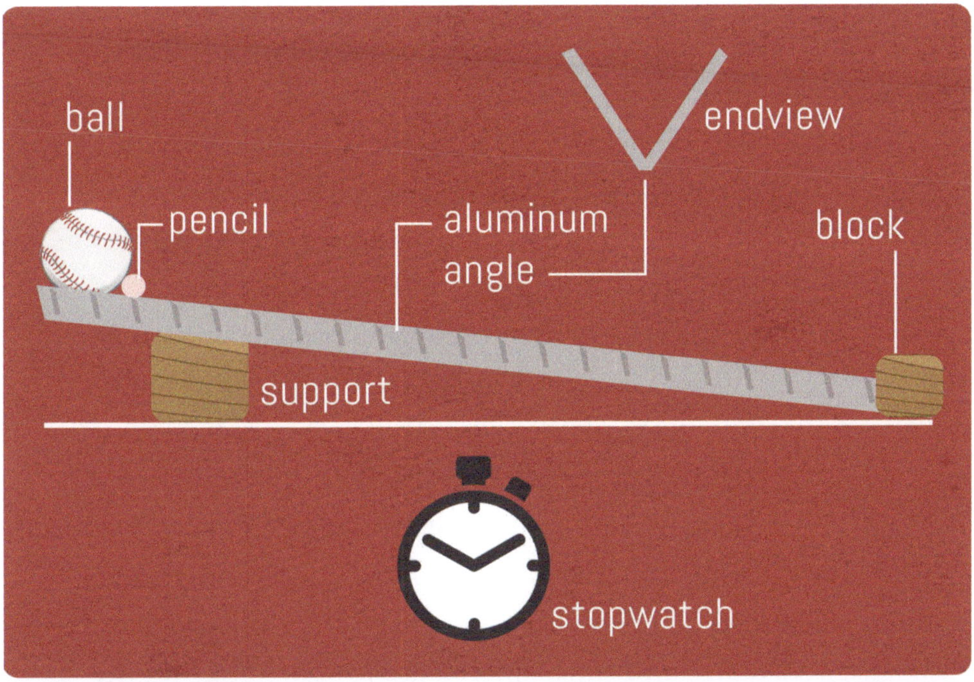

Figure 23. The drawing shows the apparatus you can use to carry out Galileo's experiment in which he diluted gravity by using an inclined plane.

1. To build a version of Galileo's inclined plane, obtain a straight, rigid, 3 m (10 ft) section of aluminum or steel angle.
2. Lay it on a floor with the "v" facing upward. Elevate one end about 15 cm with pieces of wood or books. This produces an incline of about 3 degrees (Figure 23). Blocks at the lower end of the ramp can keep the V upright.
3. Mark off 20 cm intervals starting from the elevated end. A hard rubber or steel ball can serve as the "falling body."

4. With a stopwatch, measure the times for the ball to roll from rest at the starting point (0 distance) to each marked distance along the incline. When you release the ball, be careful not to give it any backspin. This is best done by putting a pencil across the front of the ball. To release the ball, simply pull the pencil forward quickly.
5. Make several runs for each distance. Record your results and find the average time for each distance.
6. According to Galileo, the distance the ball "fell," if it accelerated at a constant rate, should be proportional to the square of the time it fell. You can check to see if this is true. For each set of distance-time data you recorded, divide the distance by the time squared. If distance and time squared are proportional, all the quotients should be about the same. For example, suppose the ball rolled 10 cm in 2 seconds and 40 cm in 4 seconds, then:

   $$\frac{10\text{ cm}}{2\text{s} \times 2\text{s}} = 2.5\text{ cm/s}^2 \text{ and } \frac{40\text{ cm}}{4\text{s} \times 4\text{s}} = 2.5\text{ cm/s}^2.$$

   Since the quotients are the same, you could conclude that the distances are proportional to the times squared.

   When the time doubles, the distance should quadruple if the acceleration is constant.
7. You can draw the same conclusion from the data in Figure 21. Plot a graph of distance traveled vs. the square of the time to travel that distance. If distance is proportional to time squared, the points you graph should lie close to a straight line.

8. What happens to the acceleration if you make the incline steeper? Less steep?

Of course, Galileo didn't have a stopwatch. He measured time by letting water fall from a vessel with a very narrow opening. The volume of water collected during the time the ball rolled was his measurement of time.

GRAVITY AND THE VALUE OF G (ACCELERATION OF A FALLING BODY ON EARTH)

Modern timing devices can measure tiny time intervals. Experiments using these devices show that over a few meters heavy objects do fall with constant acceleration. Because earth's gravity varies slightly from place to place, the actual value of the acceleration due to gravity depends slightly on location. At the Panama Canal, close to the equator, the acceleration is 9.782 m/s/s. Acceleration is slightly greater at earth's poles. At the North Pole it is 9.832 m/s/s. In New York and Chicago it is 9.803 m/s^2. The reason for this variation is that the earth is not a perfect sphere. It bulges slightly at the equator. Consequently, Earth's north and south poles are closer to Earth's center than its equator. Generally, the acceleration due to Earth's gravity is referred to as "g" and is usually expressed with two significant figures—9.8 m/s^2.

For any mass, its weight is due to the force of gravity, which would cause it to accelerate downward at 9.8 m/s^2. Therefore, the weight of a mass is ***mg***. For most purposes, g is equal to 9.8 m/s^2 or, in engineering units, 32 ft/s^2.

COMPLICATIONS WITH UNITS

To avoid using the slug, which is the engineering unit for mass, engineers use pounds (lbs) as their unit of force. When pounds are used as the unit of mass, the weight is divided by g (32 ft/s^2) so that

$$F = \frac{W}{32\ \text{ft/s}^2} \times a = \frac{\text{mg (in pounds)}}{\text{g}} \times a.$$

When a equals g, as it does with a weight, we have

$$F = \frac{W}{g} \times g = W.$$

This way the mass of a pound of weight is 1/32 of a pound.

The use of different measurements can be very confusing and cause huge practical problems. For example, NASA once lost a 125 million dollar Mars orbiter when the engineering group used the English system of measurements, while everyone else on the team used the metric system!

The United States is in a state of transition that sometimes makes measurements confusing. We use pounds for weight, but medicines are measured in grams (g) and milligrams (mg) and soda volumes are measured in liters or milliliters (mL), while milk is measured in pints, quarts, and gallons.

TERMINAL VELOCITY OF FALLING BODIES

When heavy masses that fall short distances or fall in a vacuum so that air resistance can be ignored, their accelerations are all 9.8 m/s^2.

When falling objects reach high speeds outside of a vacuum, friction with the air can be as great as the force of gravity. When this occurs, the body no longer accelerates downward but reaches a ***terminal velocity***—a velocity that does not increase further. This is what happens to skydivers who jump out of airplanes. They spread their bodies to increase contact with the air and reach a terminal velocity of about 190 kph (120 mph).

EXPERIMENT 23

GALILEO'S INVESTIGATION OF A PENDULUM

While seated in church one day, Galileo noticed a large chandelier that was swinging slowly back and forth. Using his pulse as a timer, he measured the period of the chandelier (the time to make one trip over and back). He found that the period was constant. But it led him to wonder, what would happen to the period if the chandelier were longer? Or shorter? Would the mass of the chandelier affect the period? How about the length of the swing?

When he returned to his laboratory he began an investigation of what is called a pendulum. You can build a pendulum quite easily. Then you can carry out experiments similar to those that Galileo performed.

THINGS YOU WILL NEED

- an adult
- sharp knife or razor blade
- tongue depressor or coffee stirrer
- thread
- high surface such as the top of refrigerator, a shelf, or door frame
- heavy metal washers
- meter stick or yardstick
- stopwatch
- tape
- metric ruler

1. **Ask an adult** to use a sharp knife or razor blade to make a slit about 2 cm long at one end of a tongue depressor or coffee stirrer. (See Figure 24a.)
2. Slide one end of a long piece of thread into the slit.
3. Tape the tongue depressor to a high surface such as the top of a refrigerator, a shelf, or a door frame (Figure 24b).
4. Tie the other end of the string to a heavy metal washer. The washer will serve as what is called the pendulum bob. Move the thread up or down until the distance between the bottom of the tongue depressor and the *center* of the washer is exactly 1.0 m (39 3/8 in). Tape the upper end of the string to the tongue depressor so that the length will not change when the bob swings.

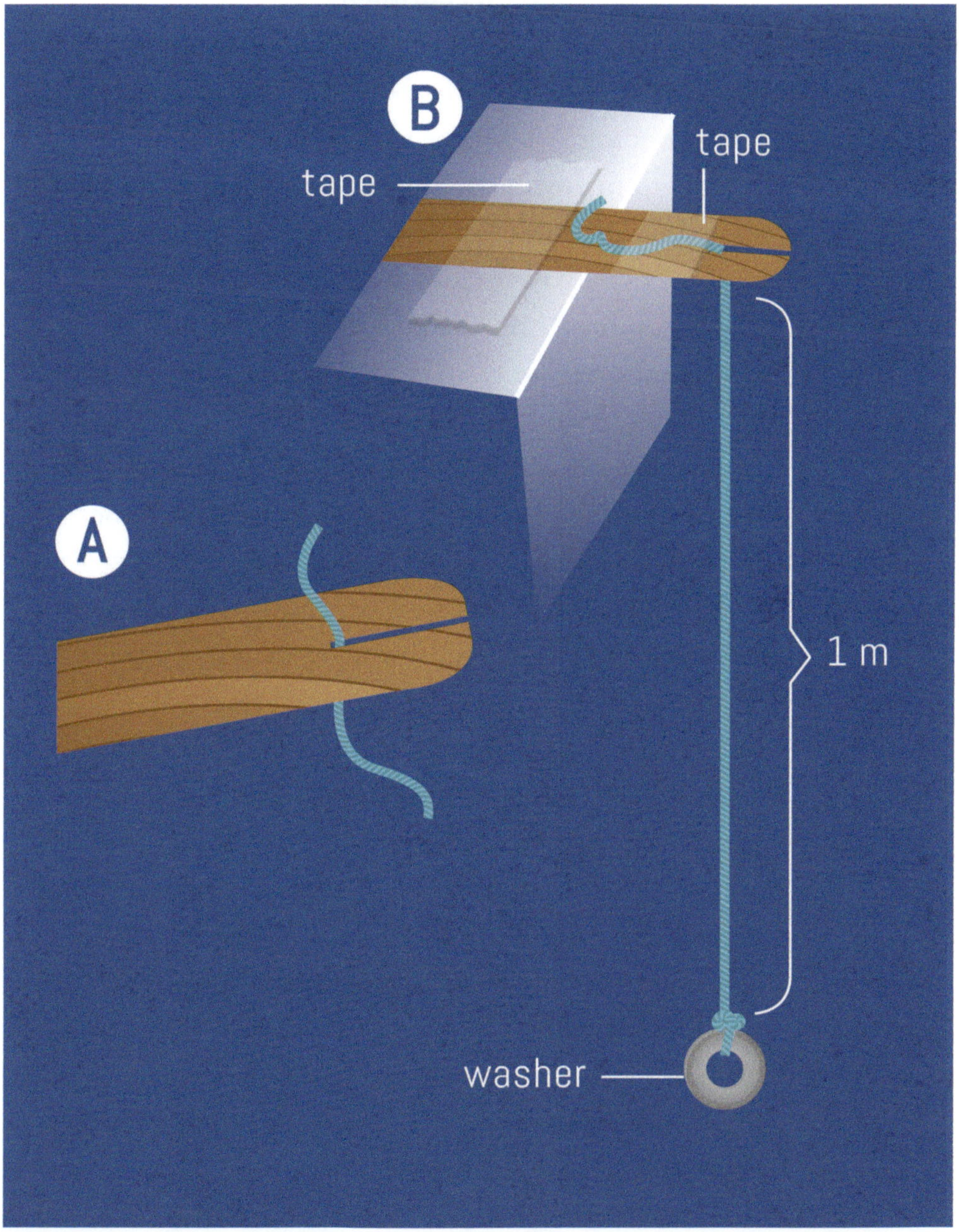

Figure 24. You can build a simple pendulum to duplicate one of Galileo's experiments.

5. Pull the washer several centimeters to one side and release it. Using a stopwatch that can measure seconds, find the time for the bob to make 10 complete swings over and back. The period of a pendulum is the time to make one complete swing, from one side to the other side and back. What is the period of the pendulum you have made? Why do you think it is more accurate to find the period by measuring 10 swings and dividing by 10 rather than timing just one swing?
6. Measure the time for the pendulum to make 20 swings. Does the period of a pendulum seem to be constant as Galileo thought it was?

When you pull a pendulum bob to one side, you also raise it a small amount. When you release it, gravity causes it to accelerate as it returns to a lower position. In the same way a toy truck will roll down an incline. Since the bob is moving when it reaches its original position, it continues to move beyond its rest position. As it rises on the other side of its swing, gravity again pulls on it causing it to decelerate, come to a stop, and swing back.

How high do you think it will rise on the other side of its swing? The swing certainly looks symmetrical, so you might think it rises to nearly the same height on both sides of its swing. One way to check is to put your nose against the bob before you release it. Don't move. Does the bob return to very nearly the point from which you released it?

HOW DOES THE MASS OF THE BOB AFFECT THE PERIOD OF A PENDULUM?

7. Will the mass of the bob affect the period of a pendulum? To find out, tape a second washer to the first one so that they are side by side.

   Repeat the experiment using the bob with twice as much mass. How does the period of this pendulum compare with the period of the lighter bob?

WHAT IS THE EFFECT OF AMPLITUDE ON THE PENDULUM'S PERIOD?

8. The amplitude of a pendulum is the horizontal distance it swings from its rest position. To test the effect of amplitude, pull the pendulum bob back 1.0 cm from its rest position. Release it and measure the period by timing 10 or more swings.
9. Measure the period when the pendulum bob is displaced 2, 4, and then 8 cm from its rest position.

   What do you conclude is the effect of amplitude on the pendulum's period?

A PENDULUM'S HALF LIFE

The half life of a pendulum can be defined as the time for its amplitude to halve.

1. To determine a pendulum's half life, build a pendulum so that the bob is very close to the floor.
2. Make a dot at the center of a sheet of paper. Then use a drawing compass to make circles with radii of 10 cm, 5 cm, and 2.5 cm.
3. With your pendulum at rest, tape the paper to the floor so that the bob's center is directly over the center of the circles. Pull the bob to the side until it is above the edge of the largest circle, 10 cm from the circle's center.
4. Release the bob and count the number of swings required for the bob to lose half its amplitude. Stop counting when the bob swings only to the 5 cm circle. Record the number of swings, which you can define as the pendulum's half life.
5. Repeat the experiment to see how many swings are required for the pendulum's amplitude to decrease from 5 cm to 2.5 cm. How does this half life compare with the first one you measured?
6. Design your own experiment to see how the mass of the bob affects the half life of a pendulum.

   Save your pendulum for the next experiment.

EXPERIMENT 24

PENDULUMS OF DIFFERENT LENGTHS

THINGS YOU WILL NEED

- an adult
- pendulum from previous experiment
- meter stick or yardstick
- stopwatch that can measure seconds
- second pendulum like one from previous experiment
- soda straw
- graph paper

1. Use the simple pendulum you built in the previous experiment to investigate the effect of length on the period of a pendulum.
2. Use a stopwatch that can measure seconds to measure the period.
3. To change the pendulum's length, pull the thread through the slit in the tongue depressor.
4. Find the period for pendulums with lengths of 1.00 m, 0.75 m, 0.50 m, 0.25 m, 1.5 m, and, if possible, 2.0 m? (or 1.00 yard, 27.0 inches, 18.0 inches, 9.0 inches, 1.50 yards and, if possible, 2.00 yards.)
5. Record the data you collect for each length.

Does the period change when the length changes? Does halving the length of a pendulum halve its period? Does doubling the pendulum's length double its period? What happens to the period when the length is one-quarter as large? What happens to the period when the length is four times as great?

6. Plot a graph of the pendulum's period vs. its length. Does the graph appear to be a straight line? Is a pendulum's period proportional to its length?
7. Next, plot a graph of the period squared vs. the length. Do the points of this graph lie reasonably close to a straight line? If they do, what does this tell you about the relationship between a pendulum's period and its length?

Engineers make good use of graphs. A graph of two variables that is a straight line indicates the variables are proportional ($y = kx$ where k is the slope of the graph).

EXPERIMENT 25

COUPLED PENDULUMS

Coupled pendulums are pendulums that are connected. They behave in interesting ways.

THINGS YOU WILL NEED

- **Two pendulums like the one in the previous experiment**
- **soda straw**

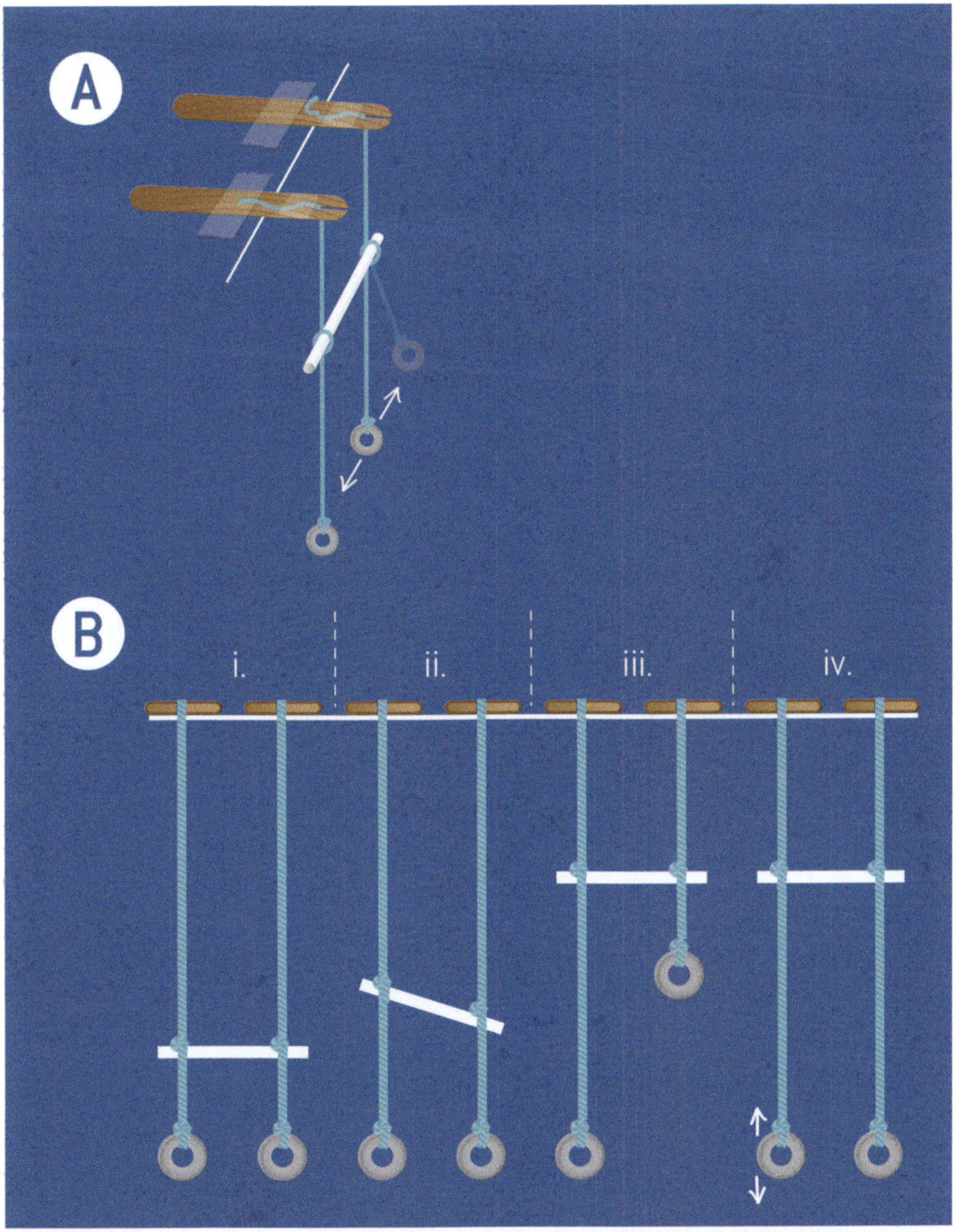

Figure 25. a) Couple two pendulums with a drinking straw. Pull one bob to the side and release it. Watch and wait. What happens to the motion? b) What happens if you i) lower the straw? ii) tilt the straw? iii) shorten one pendulum? iv) start the bob with back and forth rather than side-to-side motion?

1. Build two simple pendulums side by side as shown in Figure 25a.
2. Use a drinking straw to connect the two pendulums. (Wrap the strings around the straw.)
3. Pull one of the bobs to one side in a direction parallel to the straw. Release the bob and watch. What happens over time? What force do you think causes the motion to be transferred from one bob to the other?
4. Repeat the experiment with the straw closer to the bobs as shown in Figure 25b(i). How does moving the straw affect the motion?
5. What happens to the motions of the bobs if the straw is tilted as in Figure 25b(ii)?

   What happens to the motions if one pendulum is longer than the other as in Figure 25b(iii)?
6. What happens if the bob is released so that it swings in a direction perpendicular to the straw as in Figure 25b(iv)?

EXPERIMENT 26

A PHYSICAL PENDULUM

A physical pendulum is one made from a single piece of rigid material, such as the pendulum in a Grandfather Clock you can make a physical pendulum from a yardstick.

THINGS YOU WILL NEED

- **an adult**
- **yardstick with a hole near one end**
- **drill**
- **nail or hook**

1. Find a yardstick with a hole close to one end or **ask an adult** to drill a hole very close to one end of a yardstick.
2. Hang the pendulum from a nail or hook.
3. Pull it to one side and release it.
4. Measure the period of this pendulum. What would be the length of a simple pendulum with the same period as the physical pendulum you just built?

EXPLORING ON YOUR OWN

- From what you know about gravity and falling objects, why would you expect the period of a pendulum not to be affected by the weight of the bob?
- As you know, falling objects accelerate because gravity is a force that pulls them downward. How can a pendulum's back and forth motion be used to measure the acceleration of falling objects?

EXPERIMENT 27

SPRINGS, FORCES, AND STRETCHES

Using this experiment, you can make the same discovery that scientist Robert Hooke made in the seventeenth century.

THINGS YOU WILL NEED

- **spring such as a screen door spring or one from an old window shade**
- **pliers**
- **hook or nail**
- **standard masses (weights): 100 g to 1 kg**
- **meter stick**
- **clothespin**
- **pen or pencil**
- **notebook**
- **graph paper**
- **a second spring different from the first**

1. Find a spring, such as one used to close screen doors or one you can remove from an old window shade. If necessary, use pliers to bend a loop at one end of the spring so that it can be hung on a hook or nail.
2. Then bend a loop on the lower end of the spring to be used as a hook. A one-kilogram mass hung from the spring should stretch it about one-quarter to one-third of its original length.
3. Fasten a meter stick near the spring as shown in Figure 26. With the meter stick in place, you can

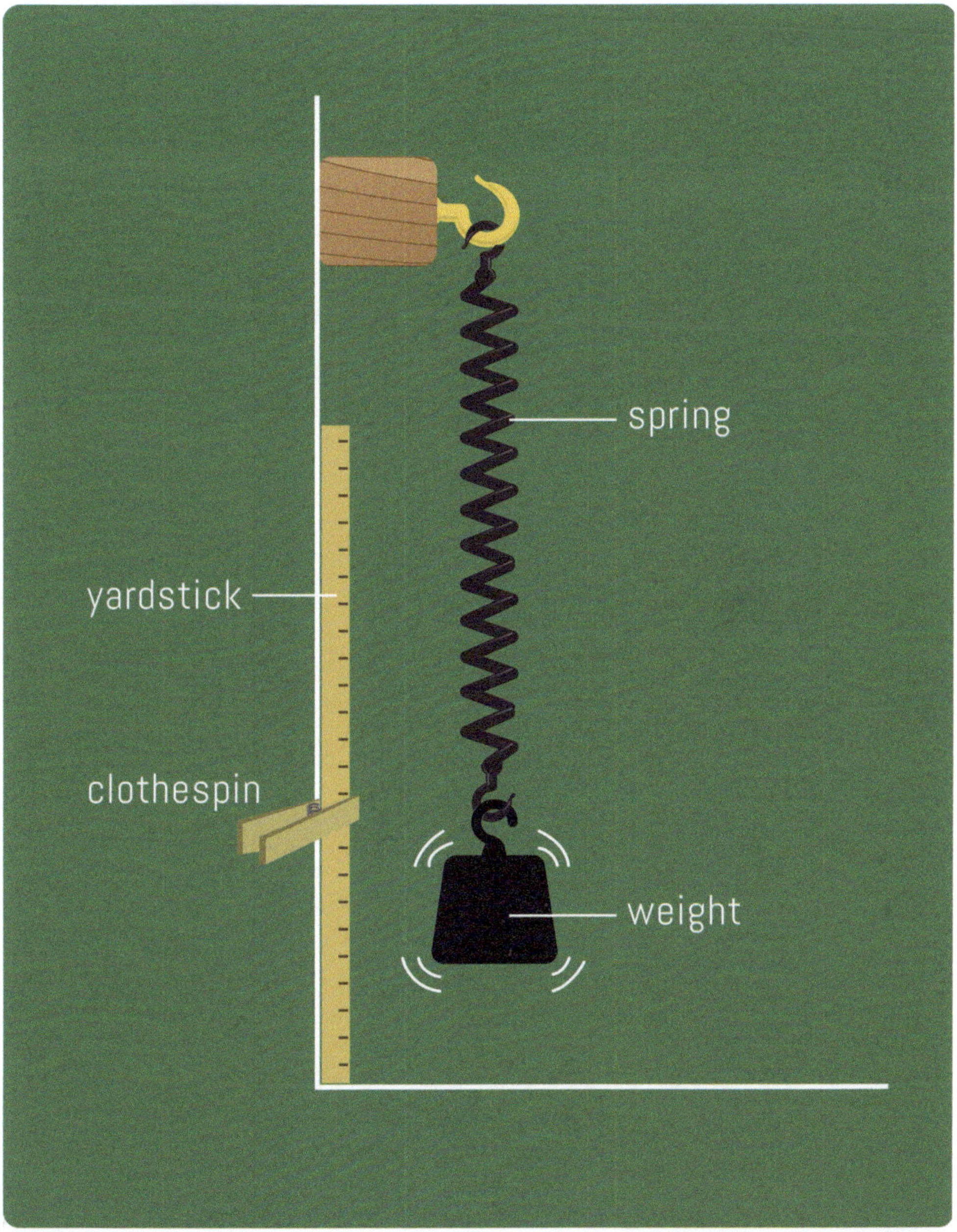

Figure 26. A spring with a mass attached can be considered a different kind of pendulum.

measure how much the spring stretches when weights are applied. A clothespin can be used to mark the spring's lowest point on the meter stick.

4. Add different masses to the spring. Measure and record the amount the spring stretches from its rest position when each mass is hung from the spring.
5. How much does the spring stretch when a 0.50 kg mass (500 g), which weighs 4.9 newtons (N) is carefully hung from it? How much does it stretch when a 1.0 kg mass (9.8 N), is hung from the spring? Record the masses and the lengths the spring stretches from its rest position.

   Does doubling the force (weight) pulling on the spring double its stretch?

   Predict how much the spring will stretch when 1.5 kg (14.7 N) is hung on the spring. Predict the amount the spring will stretch when 0.25 kg (2.45 N) is hung on the spring.
6. Test your predictions and record your measurements. Were your predictions correct?
7. Using the data you have collected, plot a graph of the force on the spring, in newtons, vs. the amount the spring is stretched, in meters.
8. Use the graph you have made to predict the amount the spring will be stretched when 100 g (0.98 N), 200 g (1.96 N), 750 g (7.35 N), and 1200 g (11.76 N) are hung from the spring. Then test your predictions. Were they correct?

9. What can you conclude about the relationship between the force on a spring and the amount the spring is stretched?

   This relationship is known as Hooke's Law. It is named for Robert Hooke, a seventeenth-century English scientist, who first discovered the law. The slope of the graph you have made, which has the units, N/m, is called the spring constant.
10. If possible, repeat the experiment with a different spring, such as one you can take from a spiral-bound notebook. With this smaller spring, you should probably use 1 newton to 5 newton (100 g to 500 g) weights. What is the spring constant for this second spring? What does the spring constant tell you about a spring's resistance to being stretched?

EXPLORING ON YOUR OWN

- Repeat Experiment 27 using smaller masses and a long rubber band in place of the spring. Does a rubber band obey Hooke's Law?
- Using what you learned in Experiment 27, explain how a spring balance works. If the markings fell off a spring balance, how would you recalibrate it? How would the spring constants for a 10 N and a 1,000 N spring balance compare?

EXPERIMENT 28

SPRINGS, AS PENDULUMS

THINGS YOU WILL NEED

- **standard masses**
- **spring and meter stick used in Experiment 27**
- **stopwatch that can measure seconds**
- **pen or pencil**
- **notebook**
- **graph paper**

Pendulums move back and forth, from side to side. Springs with a "bob" attached do something similar, but the spring's bob moves up and down.

1. Hang a 1.0 kg mass on the spring you first investigated in Experiment 27. Lift the mass about 5 cm above its rest position and let it fall. As you can see, the weight rises and falls (oscillates) in a way that appears to have a fixed period, like a pendulum. Does this motion have a fixed period?
2. To find out use a stopwatch that can measure seconds to find the time for the mass to move to its lowest position and back up to its starting position 10 times. Then measure the time for the mass to make 20 oscillations.

3. Calculate the period for both 10 and 20 oscillations. Does the motion have a constant period? If it does, what is the period in seconds?

   You probably found that the mass of the bob does not affect the period of a pendulum. Does it affect the period of an oscillating spring?

4. To find out, hang a 0.5 kg mass from the spring. Measure and record the period of the oscillating spring. Has it changed? Does halving the mass halve the period?
5. You know the period of the spring for masses of 1.0 kg and 0.5 kg. Now find the period of the oscillating spring for masses of 0.20 kg, 0.70 kg, 1.20 kg, and 1.5 kg as well.

Use the data you collect to plot a graph of the spring's period vs. the mass suspended from the spring. Do your data points form a straight line? If not, try plotting the square of the period vs. the mass. Does doubling the mass double the square of the period? Does tripling the mass triple the square of the period? What do you find? What can you conclude?

EXPLORING ON YOUR OWN

- Repeat Experiment 28 using smaller masses and a long rubber band in place of the spring. Is the square of the period of oscillation of the rubber band doubled when the suspended mass doubles?

- Measure the length of an unstretched spring. Then hang masses from the spring until it is stretched by one-third its original unstretched length. At this point, let the mass oscillate up and down. You will find that after moving up and down a few times, the spring begins to swing like a pendulum. Then it returns to its up and down motion. What happens next? Try to develop an explanation for the spring's strange behavior.

CHAPTER SIX

PROJECTS FOR YOUNG FUTURE ENGINEERS

Engineers are often asked to solve problems. Solving problems may involve research as well as thoughtful analysis and construction of models. Often engineers meet in a group to exchange thoughts and ideas. As a future engineer, you may want to do some or all of those things as you grapple with some of these projects.

- Do some research. Find Galileo's description of his experiment using an inclined plane. Then see if you can, as closely as possible, duplicate his equipment and his results.
- A question to ponder: You have found that without air resistance, light and heavy objects fall with the same acceleration. Yet, the gravitational force on a more massive object is greater than on a less massive object. Why then do they fall with the same acceleration?
- Tape a metal washer to the exact center of a file card. Tape an identical washer to one end of another file card. Hold both cards face down at the same height

above the floor. Release them at the same time. Which card reaches the floor first? Why does one card fall faster than the other?

- You probably know that submarines have periscopes. The periscopes allow the ship to remain submerged while someone looks to see what's going on in the air above the water.

  Use mirrors and whatever else is needed to build a periscope of your own design. At what angle will you arrange the mirrors relative to one another?
- Design and build a balance as sensitive as the one you made in Experiment 8 but with a larger range of measurements.
- Design and build an equal-arm balance that can weigh a paper clip as well as a pint of water.
- Put one end of a board on one bathroom scale and the other end on a second bathroom scale. Record the readings on both scales when a partner stands at different places on the board. What do you find?

  Are the results different if you move the scales to different places under the board?

  Are the results different if you lie on the board?
- Mobiles are made of multiple levers. They combine art, science, and engineering. Use wires, thread, and various small objects to build a mobile. Let your imagination and the lever principles you've investigated serve as guides.

- Gather together a piece of copper wire, a flashlight bulb, and a D-cell. With only those three items, make the bulb emit light.
- Once you have succeeded in lighting the bulb, go on to a more challenging project. Use whatever is needed to build a flashlight. Then make a circuit diagram to show how the flashlight works.
- Obtain a box of cereal. Measure the dimensions of the box. What is the volume of the box? What is the surface area of the box? What is the ratio of the box's surface area to its volume?

  Calculate and build a box that would hold the same volume of cereal but would use the least amount of cardboard.

  Could the box be made using a single piece of cardboard? If so what would be its shape? If it can be made with one piece, draw a diagram to show what it would look like. Include dimensions.

  Do you think the cereal company would buy this idea? It would require less cardboard. Therefore, their cardboard costs would be reduced. Are there other factors to consider in addition to the cost of cardboard? If so what are they? In the workforce, engineers have to think about both scientific and practical factors.
- What happens to the ratio of surface area to volume as a shape gets larger? As a shape gets smaller? Why

are babies often covered with blankets even when adults are in T-shirts?

- Design an inclined plane that would enable a wheelchair and its occupant to be safely wheeled up to a front door.
- Investigate the effect of amplitude on the period of a pendulum by continuing to increase the amplitude to its maximum value. What do you find? Does the period remain the same for very large amplitudes?
- When did clock makers recognize that pendulums could be used as clocks? What modifications did they have to make for such clocks to be practical?

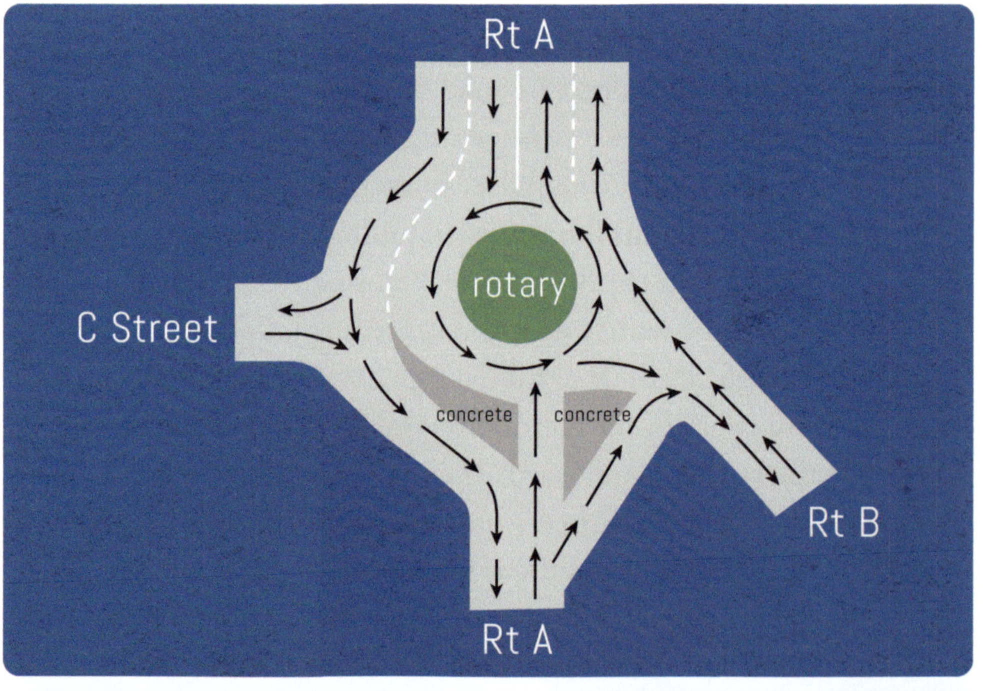

Figure 27. The diagram shows a rotary that was constructed to make it easier and safer to go from route B (Rt B) to C street. Arrows show the paths cars may take as they enter or circumvent the rotary.

- What is a Foucault Pendulum? What is its significance? Can you build one?
- Figure 27 shows a rotary that was constructed to make it easier and safer to go from route B (Rt B) to C street. Can you, as a future civil engineer, design a better solution using either a different rotary (roundabout) or some other solution such as stop lights, stop signs, overpass, underpass, or some other method?

As a future civil engineer, how would you improve this section of highway? (Cars in the rotary have the right of way.)

* ANSWER TO PROBLEM ONPAGE 81:

The velocity, v_1, between 44.1 cm and 78.4 cm is:

$$v_1 = \frac{78.4\text{ cm} - 44.1\text{ cm}}{0.1\text{ s}} = \frac{34.3\text{ cm}}{0.1\text{ s}} = 343\text{ cm/s}$$

Velocity, v_2, between 44.1 cm and 78.4 cm is:

$$v_2 = \frac{122.5\text{ cm} - 78.4\text{ cm}}{0.1\text{ s}} = \frac{44.1\text{ cm}}{0.1\text{ s}} = 441\text{ cm/s}$$

$$a = \Delta v / \Delta t = \frac{441\text{ cm/s} - 343\text{ cm/s}}{\Delta t} = \frac{98\text{ cm/s}}{0.1\text{ s}} = 980\text{ cm/s}^2 = 9.8\text{ m/s}^2$$

GLOSSARY

acceleration—A change in velocity divided by the time for the change to take place.

accelerometer—A device that can detect acceleration.

bearings—Spherical objects that turn causing a reduction in friction.

center of mass—The point where all the mass of an object can be considered to be located. It is also the balance point of an object about which clockwise and counterclockwise moments of force are equal.

friction—A force between surfaces that acts against the motion of one surface over another.

fulcrum—The point or line about which a lever turns.

g—The acceleration of falling masses near Earth's surface. The acceleration is caused by Earth's gravitational attraction for masses. The value of g is approximately 9.8 m/s^2.

gravity—The force of attraction between masses. On Earth it is the force with which Earth's mass attracts other masses.

lever—A simple machine that makes work easier or changes the direction of a force. There are three kinds of levers, first-class, second-class, and third-class.

machine—A tool that can do work.

mass—The mass of an object is the amount of matter it contains.

moment of force—A force causing something to turn times the lever arm (the distance between the fulcrum and the force.

surface area—The surface of an object in square units such as square inches (in^2) or square centimeters (cm^2).

volume—The amount of space occupied by something. It is usually measured in cubic units such as in^3, cm^3, liter, quarts, etc.

weight—The force on a mass caused by gravitational attraction. On Earth, weight is equal to mg—the mass of an object times its acceleration due to gravity.

work—A force times the distance through which the force acts.

FURTHER READING

BOOKS

Baine, Celeste. *Is There An Engineer Inside You?: A Comprehensive Guide to Career Decisions in Engineering.* Springfield, OR: Engineering Education Service Center, 2013.

CK-12 Engineering: An Introduction for High School. Palo Alto, CA: CK-12 Foundation, 2012.

Ebner, Aviva. *Engineering Science Experiments.* New York: Chelsea House Publishers, 2011.

Kuprenas, John. *101 Things I Learned in Engineering School.* New York: Grand Central Publishing. 2013.

Landis, Raymond. *Studying Engineering: A Road Map to a Rewarding Career.* Los Angeles: Discovery Point Press, 2013.

WEBSITES

MIT Open Courseware

ocw.mit.edu/high-school/engineering/

MIT's open resources for high school students interested in engineering.

National Science Foundation

nsf.gov/news/classroom/engineering.jsp

Age specific engineering activities and resources.

CAREER INFORMATION

Automationtechies
automationtechies.com/career-advice-for-young-engineers/
Career advice for aspiring engineers.

Big Future
bigfuture.collegeboard.org/majors-careers
A career and job-based website with a focus on college majors.

Electrical Engineering Schools
electricalengineeringschools.org/engineer-resources/
Numerous resources and links for electrical engineering.

Resources Pre-College
dedicatedengineers.org/Resources/pre-college_resources.htm
Great collection of links for pre-college engineers.

Salary.com
www1.salary.com/Engineering-Salaries.html
Description of salary expectations for various kinds of engineers.

Science Pioneers
sciencepioneers.org/students/stem-websites
Links to various STEM career websites

Try Engineering
tryengineering.org/become-an-engineer
Links to a wide variety of engineering careers.

U.S. News
usnews.com/education/blogs/professors-guide/2009/12/02/10-tips-for-success-for-engineering-students-
An article with some quick tips for potential engineers.

INDEX

A

B

C

Y